MW01034812

GENERATION
INTUITIVE

A Guide to Nurturing
Your Child's Infinite Potential

JULIE HAMILTON

BLUE ANGEL GALLERY
AUSTRALIA

Dedication

This book is for my mother, who fiercely encouraged my imagination and sense of wonder and in doing so pushed wide open the door to my intuition and all the gifts that lay within. I miss her every day.

Generation Intuitive:
A Guide to Nurturing Your Child's Infinite Potential

Copyright © 2008 Julie Hamilton

All rights reserved. Other than for personal use, no part of this book may be reproduced in any way, in whole or part without the written consent of the copyright holder or publisher. None of the information contained within this book is intended to replace medical assistance or treatment.

Published by Blue Angel Gallery, Australia
80 Glen Tower Drive, Glen Waverley
Victoria, Australia 3150
Phone: +61 3 9574 7776
Fax: +61 3 9574 7772
E-mail: tonicarmine@optusnet.com.au
Website: www.blueangelonline.com

Cover photographs supplied by iStock Photo
except bottom left photo by Greg Bartley featuring Nathan Avery and Edie Bartley
Treasure chest illustration by Mike Badman
Edited by Tanya Graham
Design & layout Copyright © 2008 Blue Angel Gallery

ISBN: 978-0-9803983-3-5

Acknowledgements

A huge thank you to my agent Selwa Anthony for all of her sage advice, help and support. Selwa is that rare thing, brilliant at what she does, passionate about how it's done and deeply caring to those she deals with.

My total appreciation too, to Toni and Tanya and all the staff at Blue Angel Gallery for their trust and patience with this manuscript!

Thank you also to my unwavering friend Deidre, who has been my travel partner through numerous intuitive adventures. Her continual encouragement, laughter and steadfastness have been one of the biggest blessings of my life.

Finally, my deep gratefulness to existence, for all of the moments, meetings and divinely guided experiences that have led me to this place and to my biggest inspiration, which is the innocence, awe and unbounded potential that I see in every child. They are my greatest teachers.

Contents

Chapter 1
Generation Intuitive

All of our children are born with the gift of intuition – a knowing that goes beyond reason and directly plugs them into their deepest wisdom and connects them with who they really are. What we have to do, as parents and carers, is to understand how intuition works and foster our kids' innate relationship with it. I believe that learning how to do this is crucial because the future will require us to exist at an intuitive level. To be successful today and tomorrow our children will need to be in touch with their intuitive selves. Indeed the future of their world may depend on it because contemporary living demands intuitive intelligence.

Intuitive intelligence gives our children the ability to make fantastic choices for themselves at every crossroad and keeps them connected to their authentic selves, so they can enjoy deeply rich and fulfilling lives. Until now, this dimension of our children's development has largely slipped under the radar because though most of us want this for our children, we don't have a clear idea of how to nurture it; not least because we weren't taught how to do this for ourselves and many of us have spent much of our lives trying to work it out. But there are practical, simple ways we can grow our children's intuition with them and it's important we do, because this aspect is so powerful it can truly transform our kids, ensuring that they reach their full potential.

Our children are much more than their bodies, their knowledge and their feelings. They are also a synthesis of never to be repeated talents and personality – a one-off force of being, a unique soul with a purpose for being here. As parents, I believe we can help our children get in touch with this purpose at the core of themselves, through their intuition, so they can discover who they are and their reason for being. We can raise beautiful, inspired individuals, who live their lives with confidence and strong direction – children who have such inner strength that they are invincible in the world. The good news is, it's not difficult to do, because our children are already born with the ability to access this essential inner guidance. The gateway to this connection is their intuition.

How your child uses their intuition will be as individual as they are; the point is that every child has sensory gifts. They may see the future, hear spirit guides or be natural healers. They may freely communicate with people who have left their bodies, channel creativity or be intuitively gifted at sport. However it reveals itself in your child, your job, as their guardian, is to let it develop and know how to deal with it when it does.

The Future is Intuitive

So why is teaching our kids how to use their intuition so essential? Well, simply because it's the way forward. The need for sensory intelligence is perhaps greater now than it has ever been. We live in a world that offers our children, more choices than we, or any other generation, have ever known. We cram more into our lifetimes than our parents and their parents put together. From the earliest age, our children are faced with a smorgasbord of options and a greater freedom to make their own decisions about how they live and who they are. By teaching children to use their sensory gifts we can show them how to trust their most important navigational aid in life – their own wisdom. Using their super-senses is the most important thing they can learn to do. In fact, how they make decisions, how they judge situations and how they keep themselves safe is all based on their ability to access their inner wisdom. Apart from being an essential life tool, it's also where we're headed. This is a generation that's opening up to its intuitive side like no other. From teenage Wicca, meditation and yoga for kids, Steiner schools and other alternative education to holistic healing and personal empowerment for children – there's a global movement to tap into more conscious ways of being for our youth. What used to be a new-age niche is now mainstream. Everywhere, there is an explosion of interest in the realms beyond our immediate experience. Terms like karma, past lives and spirit guides are now part of our everyday language, shows featuring young witches and psychic detectives are now showing during prime time television and exploration of fields such as Quantum Physics as well as a vast array of alternative medicines are changing the way we perceive the world in which we live. Our children are growing up in a time where the metaphysical and the physical are no longer seen as separate. Society is undergoing radical transformation.

And it's into this ground-swell of change that children I call 'Generation Intuitives' or 'Gen I's' are being born. This is a time where being able to tap into our higher consciousness is becoming essential. Our kids are growing up on a planet that's demanding, complex and changing at an exponential rate. As it changes, their way of being in the world must inevitably expand. As our global culture metamorphoses, so does the next generation of its citizens. It's no coincidence that as we move into an age where there is a deep need for six-sensory living, our children are being born equipped with greater sensitivity to the world of intuition. Gen I's are reflecting this awakening by coming in with the tools to deal with the new order. I call these children 'Generation Intuitives'. It's intuitive evolution.

The Intuitive Tribe

There is a new zeitgeist and Generation Intuitive is arriving at a watershed time in our evolution where attitudes are changing rapidly. Sociologist, Paul H. Ray, and Psychologist, Sherry Ruth Anderson, have extensively researched this wave of change in their book, *The Cultural Creatives: How 50 Million People Are Changing the World*. They describe a new tribe of young people with a love of nature and an awareness of our planet's ecological issues, who are environmentally aware and politically savvy consumers. These are teenagers and twenty-somethings who consider spirituality to be important in their lives but are concerned about religious fundamentalism, who care about social issues, education and sustainability but who are disenfranchised by current politics and want to find a new effective way of government. Cultural Creatives are optimistic and distrust the pessimism in the media, they choose abundance but reject materialism – they tend not to be in debt and are against rampant globalism. They are interested in personal development, women's issues and exploring notions of community while remaining highly independent. There is a new paradigm that simultaneously seeks connectedness and individuality.

They value conscious relationships with themselves and others. They reject old conditioning around race, sexuality and religion while embracing different ethnicities, spiritual practices and expressions of love, as being equal and valid. Most significantly, Cultural Creatives value their own internal compass rather than external values in deciding how to live their lives. This group is defined by its tendency to live intuitively – to consult the inner for outer direction.

The New Attitude is Intuitive

Teaching our kids how to live intuitively is about helping them keep pace with the sensory evolution that's taking place. And there are some other pressing reasons to get in the intuitive know. Intuitive kids become successful adults. When our children learn how to plug into their highest wisdom, they can make great choices and live their lives with joy and purpose. When our sons and daughters live intuitively, they have a personal relationship with their essence, with who they truly are, and they become more connected with everything and everyone around them. It allows them to move to a place of unlimited potential, a boundless and energetic landscape where they can be all they can be, in every way. Living intuitively gives them the best chance they have of being safe, powerful and creative in their lives.

Intuition and Keeping our Kids Safe

One of the most important reasons to help our children use their intuition is because it's one of the greatest protections we can give them. We live in a world where absolutely nothing is reliable – there are no guarantees that any situation is entirely free from danger or that anything will remain constant. Everyone can get sick or hurt or be disappointed. Places and people can be destroyed or damaged. The harsh reality for parents is that no matter how much we might try to prevent our children from experiencing any type of pain, ultimately we are powerless to stop it. What we can do however, is make our children powerful in the face of the curve balls that life throws at them. Children who know they can rely on their intuition – what they know to be true inside – regardless of what is happening externally, have the strongest foundation possible. Giving children this rock-solid base is the best thing we can do for them, because it's from this place of trust in themselves, rather than from a place of fear, doubt or defensiveness, that they make the best choices and relate to their environment and others in a balanced, whole way.

For example, if a child is being told by their intuition that they have landed in a potentially dangerous situation and need to get out, and they listen to that and act on it, then they learn to trust themselves. Every time they heed that inside knowing their self-esteem grows. Every time they don't listen to that voice or trust it, they abandon themselves because their intuition is their very core.

If you leave a child on their own they quickly learn that they can't trust you, and it's the same with our intuition. When we walk away from our own wisdom, we immediately sense that we are not safe. It's so critical for kids to understand that they can trust their intuition because when the going gets tough, when they hit a crisis, when they feel they are in a situation there is no way out of, or when they feel overwhelmed, it's this trust of their inner voice that's going to get them through.

We can teach our children to come to us or their teachers or a respected person in the community, for help and advice. That's very worthwhile – we all need an outside take on things, and to be able to ask for help and receive wisdom from people with more experience than us. But ultimately, even the decision to accept or act on this wisdom has to come from a place inside. If we can put our kids in touch with that inner knowing of what is right for them, not only will they be able to make the majority of decisions for themselves, they will also know when they need to use the resources of others.

In this way, intuition is a never-ending well of guidance. Teaching our children to use their intuition also energetically immunises them from the role of victim. Because intuition is endlessly creative and boundless, it will always give them options regardless of how desperate or hopeless the circumstances they find themselves in. The knowledge that they can trust themselves and that they have power, regardless of what's happening in their world, is enough on its own to empower children to live a fulfilling life. I think that's very exciting – and I know I want it for my kids. But there are even more fabulous reasons for teaching our kids to expand their intuition.

Intuition and Creativity

Intuition and creativity are inextricably linked. If we want our children to live successful and fulfilling lives they must use their creativity. When I talk about creativity here, I don't mean that our children must grow into artists and writers and dancers – though fantastic if they do. I mean creativity in the widest sense. You can be a creative welder, banker or stay-at-home mum. Our intuition wants us to continually grow and expand, and to experience our world and our existence in new and exciting ways. In every moment we have a choice about how that's going to look – and that's a lot of choices every day. How our children choose their direction and deal with opportunity depends on how well they are connected to their intuition. Intuition is, in its nature, like creativity. It's free flowing, it's unlimited in the ways it can reveal itself to us and its insight or guidance can lead us to push boundaries, make new discoveries and take risks. Creativity and intuition go hand in hand.

The remarkable thing about intuition is that it leads each of us, personally, to never-ending possibilities that are only perfect for us. In this way, our intuition and creativity are as individual as we are. Intuition then, is essential if we want our children's lives to become a unique expression of who they are. The wonderful thing is that because their intuition and creativity are so unique and personal, there is no need for them to compete with others. We can teach our kids that what they have to offer is endlessly valuable and original. They never have to feel jealous or less than anyone else, because if they are in touch with their intuition they will create something with their lives that is unrepeatable. If a child is not in tune with their intuition, their creativity will inevitably be stunted. Their personal choices will be limited to what they perceive is possible. In contrast, a child living an intuitive life has endless horizons because intuition comes from a vast consciousness. They can experience the ultimate beauty of living as an expression of complete creativity and allow their intuition to guide them to that.

Intuition and Destiny

If living a safe and creative life don't seem like good enough reasons to nurture your child's intuition, there is one other compelling reason to do so. And that is that our intuition will reveal to us our life's purpose.

Every child that is born has a purpose on this planet. Life might appear to be chaotic and contradictory but intuition shows us there is a bigger plan. If our children know this from a young age, their lives will be radically different. Firstly they will live their lives with a sense of meaning. They will understand that everything that happens to them is happening for a reason because it helps them to progress further down their pre-chosen path. The benefits of seeing existence in this way are huge. Firstly, it removes any sense of meaninglessness, protecting children against depression and hopelessness. It also gives kids an understanding that they have a direction even if they don't initially know what it is, and that they have a unique contribution to make which virtually Teflon-coats them against low self-esteem. Seeing life from the perspective that 'we're here to learn something and make a unique contribution' also makes it a big adventure. If they can get a handle on their destiny, then they can walk in sync with it, rather than against it. So, as they get older, they will be in a masterful position where all their choices and actions will be in line with where they want to go – now, that's the kind of power I want for my kids, don't you? The best part about this power is it helps children to directly experience how they can co-create their reality – that they can actually make the things they want happen in their life, just by aligning with their purpose and following their intuition.

The happiest and most successful people I have ever met all say that they knew where they were headed from an early age. In the years that I have spent helping people to discover their destiny, the most common reason I've found for people to be clueless as to what they should be doing in work and love is that they rarely tune into their intuition. The value of helping a child to start to explore why they are here is priceless. When, as adults, we don't feel we are in touch with our destiny and know where we are going, we often experience a great deal of resentment and frustration. If children are shown how to use their intuition, they can bypass this entirely. Children who are in an environment where their intuition is allowed to blossom will inevitably gravitate towards their heart's desire. They will be drawn to investigate their passion. Children who know what they love and have the courage to pursue it are potential world champions. And what better reason to use your intuition than to create a successful and fulfilling life?

Intuitive Pioneers – the New Parenting Paradigm

So we can see that teaching our children to use their intuition is essential and that the sooner we get started, the better because as we all know, the time to teach kids is when they're, well, kids! And yes, they do seem to grow up very fast nowadays – ten is the new twenty!! But if you have no idea about how to do it, don't worry, you are not alone.

We are the first generation of parents to be dealing with this subject in such a deep way, largely, because we are being asked to keep up with a new breed of intuitive pioneers. This is ground-breaking stuff – we didn't get a guidebook in the labour ward and no-one showed us how to do it when we were growing up. Many of us are exploring, for the first time, this part of ourselves – never mind getting our heads around teaching our kids about it! But the beauty of this process of discovery is that everyone benefits; as our kids transform, so do we. The old saying, 'we teach what we most need to learn,' couldn't be more appropriate. In fact, the call to parent our intuitive children inevitably means we have to be open to taking on board some new knowledge.

I want to acknowledge upfront that parenting from an intuitive perspective takes courage. It asks us to open into the unknown, experiment and let things unfold. It often means being taken out of familiar realms and for that reason we may encounter things that we do not immediately understand, agree with or like. Nurturing our kids' intuition as parents means letting go of ideas of control and thoughts about what's right. It's personally, socially and politically challenging because intuition goes beyond conventional morality or social mores, which change rapidly and are consistently either re-worked or completely rejected by each succeeding generation.

One of the most immediate challenges for parents of Gen I children is that dealing with this whole new frontier in parenting requires a degree of trust, because intuition is something that's largely outside the scope of rational explanation. Osho, the revolutionary Indian mystic and teacher describes this quandary perfectly in his book, *Intuition: Knowing beyond Logic*, when he says, "Intellect is involved with the known and the unknown, not with the unknowable. And intuition works with the unknowable, with that which cannot be known... Intuition cannot be explained scientifically because the very phenomenon is unscientific and irrational."

That's a confronting concept, largely because our contemporary culture places enormous emphasis on logic and requires things to be proven or demonstrated before they can be trusted. It wasn't always so. Historically our communities made choices by taking part in a variety of shamanic, pagan and magical practices, consulting wise men and women elders, or drawing on the rituals of different spiritual traditions. With the arrival of organised religion and the birth of scientific enquiry, these traditions were largely seen as ignorant superstitions which belonged to the dark ages. The brave new world of medicine, philosophy and research brought enormous social, technological and economic advancement. But the new leaps in knowledge came at the expense of a vast warehouse of wisdom. Instead of taking the valuable parts of the old ways and incorporating them into our new knowledge, we dumped them altogether. We swung 180 degrees and anything which was seen as unknowable or beyond reason was viewed with scepticism. As a result, we now live in a world where intuition has a bad reputation and is grossly devalued. For a long time, intuition has been perceived as the eccentric currency of a new-age niche instead of the valuable resource that it is. The bottom line is we still need to bring things back into balance and intuition works whether or not we understand the mechanics of it. What we do need to do is demystify much of the thinking around intuition. It might sound like a contradiction in terms but there's a great deal of common sense that can be applied to intuition, even if it is intangible.

In fact, what we know about intuition is increasing at a swift rate. I believe it's no coincidence that it's now, at this point in our evolution, where our knowledge and understanding is expanding exponentially, that Gen I's are coming into our homes and hearts. Yet despite the changes in consciousness that are occurring, the suspicion that surrounds intuition still affects us. The source of intuition is still contentious and so, there is still a lot of doubt and anxiety attached to it. Given the climate of disbelief around intuition that still exists, it's hardly surprising that we often disregard it ourselves or encourage our children to do so. Regardless of whether we ignore it or not, all of us have experienced the phenomenon of intuition in our lives. We may call it instinct or a gut feeling and we may not ever have thought about it or where it comes from, but we have all sensed it. Ironically, although intuition is beyond the rational mind, its defining nature is the clear knowing that it brings. Intuition is a mystery but we can harness its power regardless.

Intuition – Getting to the Source

If we are going to help our children develop their unique abilities, then we need to understand what being intuitive means.

It's my experience when kids use their intuition they are tapping into their soul or source, basically that part of them that is unparalleled and unlimited. Simultaneously they are also accessing a universal consciousness, part of a divine order, over-soul or oneness. I think of it as connecting with a universal matrix, or 'all that is'. Intuition comes to us from beyond our beliefs, our conditioning, our ego and values. It's paradoxically us, and yet beyond us. As Osho states, "Intuition can give you the answer to ultimate questions". "Intuition leads you only to yourself, hence its beauty, its freedom and its independence.""It is an exalted state needing nothing." For our children, being on close terms with their intuition is an opportunity to know themselves beyond the confines of their physical world. For this to be possible, they have to first be able to identify it when it shows itself. Fortunately intuition has some defining features, which make it easy to recognise.

Intuition – the Low Down

• It can be trusted – it always has our best interests at heart. Intuition does not give us a bum steer; it comes exclusively from a position of love, protection and respect for us.
• It is a super-sense, additional to our five basic senses, and using it simultaneously boosts our other senses.
• It always speaks the truth, though not necessarily the truth as we choose to see it – sometimes our super-sense speaks from places we would rather ignore!
• Our intuitive experience is incredibly personal – it's expressed in a highly individual way.
• Information that comes from our super-sense is objective; it comes without pressure, expectations or 'shoulds'.
• While intuition may (especially in cases of emergency) give us information that includes other people, it predominantly speaks of what is best for us alone.
• It comes to us at a deeper level than the intellect. It is free of doubt, fear and anxiety, which are all the hallmarks of mind-talk.
• Intuition makes us feel certain and gives us clarity.
• It speaks to us in a way we can understand or learn to understand.
• It's universal.
• It comes to us without effort.
• It never leaves us. We can dip into it at any time and it never runs out.
• The more we use it, the stronger it gets and the easier it is to access.

- All the direction we receive is within our power to achieve.
- It leaves us with a deeper connection to ourselves, others and our world.
- Intuition offers us a new way of experiencing our reality.
- It increases our sensory perception.
- It's highly creative and boosts our own creativity.
- It helps us grow as beings.

Intuition is a powerful force for guidance and self-knowledge, even if our awareness of it is limited and we experience it only at a very basic level. The challenge for parents of Gen I's is to know how to allow this part of our children to flower. This is especially tricky, given that every child is different and how they will express their intuition is as individual as they are.

As in every other area of childhood, kids develop at varying rates. Gen I's can be found at every point on the intuitive spectrum. Your child may be what I describe as 'sensory gifted,' that is, easily able to tune into their intuitive self — often in exceptional ways. If this doesn't sound like your child, but you know that your child is sensitive to intuition, then it's likely that all they need is support and encouragement to open into their sensory potential. Wherever your child is at in relation to their intuition they will have particular needs, each requiring its own response. One level of intuitive awareness is not better than another and they all have challenges for the child and the parents. There is no evidence to suggest that children who are slower to open to their intuition are less skilful in the long run. In fact, there are often important reasons why they may be slower to start — these will be discussed later on. Interestingly, sensory gifted children show many parallels to academically gifted children, who often surge ahead while young, but usually plateau as they hit adulthood. The point is that it's not a race and the secret is to work at their pace. You can't hot-house intuition. The ultimate goal is to find what works for that child, as intuition is a unique expression of the individual it comes from. Every child can learn to use their intuition to the extent to which they are comfortable — the trick is to work at their speed.

This book and the exercises in it are designed for all children, regardless of where they are at. It's been written to show how we can help all our children realise what they are truly capable of, and expand and harness their inimitable talents.

Chapter 2
Intuitive Childhood

How much is your child using their intuition now? To help identify where your child is at, right now, with their intuition, read this list and see which of these things applies to your child, noting whether it's been once, occasionally or often.

My child:

1. Sees angels, spirits, energy or auras.
2. Glimpses the past or future beyond what they could logically know.
3. Hears the voices of spiritual guides, angels and/or people, alive or dead.
4. Has a deep knowing about things that are outside their knowledge or understanding.
5. Communicates with beings that are outside physical form.
6. Shows an incredible connection with nature and animals and relates with them at a level that goes deeper than words.
7. Talks about or practices healing on pets, toys, friends (imaginary or real) and siblings through touch or just by thinking about it.
8. Shows wisdom way beyond their years or reckoning.
9. Is very creative and has a great imagination – their play world reflects original ways of seeing or thinking about things.

10. Is deeply fascinated by magical stories and characters.

11. Discusses God/the divine/universal energy as if they have a personal relationship.

12. Is highly curious about spiritual matters and talks about them frequently.

13. Regularly has powerful dreams.

14. Accesses inner guidance easily.

15. Senses the world intensely through their body, emotions or thoughts.

16. Is/has been attracted to crystals.

17. Seems to have a strong energetic presence.

If you have ticked at least three or more, your child is probably already quite tuned in with their intuition and using it a lot. If your child doesn't seem to be using their intuition very much at the moment then it may be time to help them tap into that innate intuitive ability.

The Sensory Gifted Kid

So let's talk first about a number of Gen I kids, who are very in tune with their intuition. They are generally not difficult to pick, because while they can show their sensory giftedness in a large range of ways, there are usually a number of similar factors that help to pick them out — often at a very early age.

Increasingly, we are the guardians of small people with impressive abilities; children who are able to tune into profound wisdom and healing, small people with an increased level of intuition and who are in touch with it. These are precious souls with valuable talents, who have much to teach us about how to be and how to intuitively evolve into the new millennium. These kids are on the intuitive superhighway. Their experience of intuition is multi-dimensional and usually multi-sensory. They are instinctive intuitives, with a totally different take on reality.

If you are a parent or carer of a sensory gifted child then you'll probably suspect it already, because even if you can't pin down why, you'll just know that they are special. So many parents I talk to feel embarrassed about admitting they think their children have sensory gifts. They are scared they'll be judged as excessively proud mums and dads – even though deep down, they know that it's true. We are often delighted to boast about our child's sporting or academic achievements but when it comes to intuition, we're much more cautious. Even if you don't feel comfortable chatting about it at the School Fete, it's important to acknowledge it for yourself. By owning it, you can move forward into dealing with it. The truth is that regardless of what they can do, they are just ordinary kids with extraordinary talents. In addition to using the five senses of touch, sight, smell, hearing and taste, they also experience the world through a heightened awareness or consciousness. There's nothing spooky or scary about these children, they are, in fact, amazingly beautiful individuals who arrive with an ability to easily access powerful wisdom, intuition and different ways of seeing. Hopefully in the near future sensory gifted children will be the norm. Until then, what we, as parents, need to learn is how to recognise and care for them.

Gen I = Supernatural

If you know you have one of these children – great! They truly are fantastic beings. There are some important reasons why Gen I's need to be discovered as soon as possible. These super-sense individuals have special needs and must be nurtured and protected because their senses are, like them, innocent, open and full of potential. For a sensory gifted child, chatting to a soul that has passed on, healing a pet or clearly seeing someone else's aura is completely normal. It's who they are. They are truly supernatural – literally, more natural than natural! Sensory gifted kids are simply doing what we all have the ability to do – the difference is they make it look easy. They are born already knowing how to do it. The challenge for parents or carers of such children is ongoing and what's needed is the knowledge to support them and to show them how to foster and be with their gifts in a positive and down-to-earth way. We need to guide them to use these gifts, help them feel great about who they are and what they can do and to view this unique ability as an incredible plus.

If your child shows less interest or confidence in the intuitive arena it's probably helpful to know that wherever a child is in relationship to their intuition has absolutely no bearing on what they are capable of. They might be a late starter or have just had no exposure to the idea of what you can do with intuition. For many kids, all it takes is for the door to the super-sensory world open and for them peek in. When they see the treasure trove inside, they will go and explore for themselves. All they need to know is how to get to the door......so let's follow the treasure map!

Gen I — Their World, Their Way

How your child experiences their intuitive world will be influenced by their age, development and where their personal strengths lie. While their intuition may manifest in many areas, frequently a child will have one, 'speciality' where they are strongest – one sense that is dominant. This can change as they grow older as either another sense takes over or others become equally as powerful. Often it's influenced by the child's own preferences; they may feel more comfortable with a one expression of their intuition over another. It's also my experience that some super-sensory gifts are more common while others are quite rare. For example, it is quite rare for children to channel information directly from spirit. Logically, this would seem to be because little people would find such an experience overwhelming. Just as we need a certain level of maturity to cope with the sensation of drinking alcohol, a few, though not many, sensory gifts, require an adult sensibility.

If you want to really understand your Gen I kid, then you need to get an idea of how they experience their intuitive world and get an inside look at what it's actually like for them. So let's really look at all the ways your child can express their intuition. Each of the following chapters will take an in-depth look into a different super-sense and will cover how it feels for a child who is already using that particular sense, what they get out of it and how to nurture and encourage that sense in your child. We'll begin with one of the most common senses – 'Super-Sight,' also known as 'Intuitive Vision.'

Chapter 3
Intuitive Vision

Intuitive vision is the visual super-sense. Of all the super-senses it is the most complex because of the large number of ways it can manifest. This chapter outlines some of the ways your child will experience the world if they express their intuition in this visual way.

The Inner Eye

When your child has access to intuitive vision, they might describe it like having a film camera inside their head. What they actually experience when they close their eyes, or more rarely with their eyes open, is a single scene or a series of images unfolding like a movie or a picture book. These pictures can be incredibly detailed and complex and, for some children, feel just as 'real' as the external world. Often these children see these images in cartoon form or as a drawing. It's important to understand that, although these children will usually be very visually creative, what they are describing is much more than a rich fantasy world. The images they see, while awake, are carry meaning or information, in a similar way to dreams. Their intuition is talking to them through the images, even if they don't immediately understand the message. Learning how to interpret what they see is a matter of practice as the images can be either very literal or symbolic.

Often it's not the actual picture but what it means to the child that counts. The experience of Dominick, aged eight, illustrates this perfectly:

"While we were playing outside on holiday last year, Dominick nearly stood on a venomous snake. Thankfully, the snake didn't attack but slithered off. Instead of being scared, Dom thought the snake had behaved like a mate by not biting him. Now when Dom is thinking about people or places and sees a snake with them, he gets a good feeling. For him it means the situation or the person isn't going to hurt him."
- Dominick's Mum, Maria.

This is a great example because the image of the snake has been used to represent wisdom, temptation, health and evil at different times in our culture. So if your child experiences intuition in this way, it's essential that you spend time to find out what the symbol or image means for them and try not to put your own interpretation on it. Needless to say there can be a lot of trial and error in this process, especially if your child is still not able to use language with sophistication – but you can have a lot of fun working it out!

Dominick's story also brings up another central issue about nurturing our children's intuition and that is, we can only help them to trust their intuition if we show them that *we* trust their view of things. Having said that, there also needs to be some common sense applied. Children don't always have enough life experience to accurately judge a situation. If you have doubts about a scenario, then take appropriate action, but wherever possible let your child experience how it feels to have made a 'good call.' Afterwards reinforce this knowing by praising them. The important thing to remember is that when intuition talks, however it talks to us, it does so for a reason. In Dominick's case, it was using pictures to show him who he could trust and how he could keep himself safe.

As mentioned earlier, kids sit on a wide intuitive spectrum. There will be some kids who access their intuition in this way every day, while for others it might be irregular or rare. If you want to encourage your kids to use their intuition in this form or to expand on what they already know, then without question guided visualisation is the most valuable exercise you can do to expand their visual intuition. There is one at the end of this

> *"It teaches your child one of the most important skills a Gen I can learn, which is that they are in control of their gifts and it's not the other way around."*

chapter, specifically written to stimulate this aspect of your child's intuition. You can use the one provided or make up your own. You might like to use pirates, wizards, unicorns or astronauts – whatever they are into – to create something that will appeal to them. The beauty of visualisation is that it's a fun activity you can share anywhere – in the car, in the doctor's waiting room or at bedtime and you can tailor it to suit your child's age and development.

If your child already uses their visual intuition a great deal, you both have a different set of challenges. The first is to help them process what they are seeing. You can do this by encouraging them to draw what they see, and then talking about the images and what they might represent. Provide a safe – neutral and non-judgemental – space for them to discuss what they see, if they want to. Let them find their own way of interpreting things.

If what they see is overwhelming or they are receiving a large amount of information and are feeling swamped, you can teach them how to switch the pictures off. Ask them to imagine a TV or movie screen in their head and tell them to take the remote control and switch it off. Explain to them they can turn it back on whenever they want to and that it will automatically come on when it has something important to broadcast. The beauty of this simple exercise is that it teaches your child one of the most important skills a Gen I can learn, which is that they are in control of their gifts and it's not the other way around.

Nurture it! Here's what you can do to help:
• Give them time and space to zone out.
• If you see them tuning in, don't interrupt them.
• Encourage them to describe what they see by painting or storytelling.
• Don't be concerned if they have strong emotional reactions to what they are seeing. If possible get them to talk or draw how they feel. Help them to

understand the link between what they see and how they feel.

• Give them regular 'visual feasts' – take them to art galleries or to see interesting architecture and design. Stimulate them visually by using picture books – there are so many great ones out there. Get a library card and wear it out! Take them to movies, the theatre and art shows. All forms of visual expression stimulate visual intuition. Let them dabble in hobbies that involve pictures. It could be anything from photography to scrap-booking. Have fun creating stories with pictures. You can make a mini-book with them or have them draw cartoons.

The major benefit of using this type of intuition is that it encourages kids to develop new ways of looking at things.

Visualisation: The Magic Forest

Close your eyes and imagine that you are standing on the edge of a thick, dark, green forest. It's very safe. If you feel unsure, you can take someone you trust along with you to hold your hand!

Walk along the narrow path in front of you. Above you, there are very tall trees stretching into the sky. Flowers of all different colours grow along the sides of the pathway, bobbing in the wind. It makes you feel happy to be here. You come to a fork in the path and it branches left and right. Which way to go? You look around and see a wise tree sprite crouching on a branch. His clothes are made of leaves sewn together by spider webs – how funny! He points his nobbly finger, showing you where to go. Was it right or left? You follow the path winding through the trees. The sun is shining between the leaves, lighting up the path as you go. You feel very peaceful. Suddenly the path opens out into a clearing and in the centre is an ancient tree, bigger and older than any other tree you have ever seen. In the centre of the tree-trunk is a doorway. You have a good look but you can't find a way to open it. Just when you are ready to give up, a white, shining Unicorn appears from behind the tree. Hanging from his shimmering horn is a key. You thank him, take the key, open the door and follow the spiral staircase inside that takes you to a room in the topmost branches. In the room is an enchanted mirror. You can look in the mirror and ask any question you like and it will always show the truth. What do you ask? And what is the answer? Can you see what it's showing you? When you are finished you go back down to the forest floor. The unicorn is waiting for you and he asks you to get on his back. You climb up and he flies you back to the edge of the forest in no time at all. He tells you, with a shake of his mane, that you can ask the mirror to show you what you need to know anytime you like.

Super-Real Perception

When children see their world intuitively, they perceive everything in an incredibly intense way. They see colours more vibrantly and register exquisite detail. This energetically enhanced vision is like looking through a magnifying glass, or seeing everything through dramatic camera filters. Often this visual intensity evokes strong feeling or emotion. Your child may start to cry while looking at a flower, or have feelings of awe in a certain building or in nature. If this happens, there is no need to be concerned; they are literally feeling the beauty of what they see. It's quite normal for children in touch with this super-sense to spend long periods of time scrutinising something we take for granted like the dust motes floating in shafts of sunlight or the plants and wildlife in the garden. They can be entirely lost in the wonder of what they are seeing and fall into a meditative or euphoric state – literally a natural high!

The purpose of this sort of intuition is not to give guidance or provide protection but rather, it connects children with a sense of awe, bliss and oneness – with all that is. In this mode of intuition children will regularly experience themselves as being open, unfettered love and potential. It's a place of acceptance and aliveness. Clearly this is a great spot to be! And if we teach our children to access it, then they can come here, when they need to recharge and remember who they really are.

I've had many experiences of this type of super-sight. The most vivid was while on a train in Europe passing slowly through the French countryside.

For nearly six hours, I watched spellbound as every blade of grass and the leaves on the trees stood out in mesmerising detail. It was as if the landscape was alive and singing to me and I could see and feel every part of the life-force in it and felt connected to it in a visceral way.

There are two distinguishing features to this type of super-sense. The first is that the direct experience of it can last much longer than any other type of intuition, sometime hours at a time. Secondly, though it can happen anywhere – out in the car or at home – it's most likely to be triggered outdoors. The reason is that the link between nature and intuition is very strong. Many spiritual teachers have spoken about the powerful connection between the world of nature and the divine. Indeed mystics have taught that time in the wilderness is a fast track to our inner selves and to spiritual enlightenment. Whether or not our kids become enlightened by being in the garden, the simple act of being outdoors has a powerful effect on their energy, actions and feelings and it will often trigger this type of intuition.

Nurture It! Here's what you can do to help:
• Create space for daydreaming. Dreamy children can drive their parents to distraction – they always seem elsewhere, especially when you have to leave for school in two minutes! But at more convenient times, day-dreaming is very important because it's during this 'time out,' when the brain is idling, that intuition has the space to show itself. When our children have checked out from their immediate world, they are often tuning in to their inner world. Looking out of the window when being driven in the car, time alone in their room or just sitting in the garden is all very valuable. If you ever come across a child lost in their own reverie, you'll notice they have a certain aura about them which is incredibly tranquil. One of the best ways to encourage daydreaming is to reduce the amount of external stimulation that they are bombarded with. So, switch off the radio, the computer, the *Playstation*, the television or whatever is filling up the space and let them wander aimlessly for a while. Boredom is actually very healthy for kids because after their initial irritation, they will naturally come up with creative responses, usually quite quickly. If they want to share the contents of their daydreams, let them. If not, respect that.
• Spend time in nature. Go camping, go for walks, get out on the water

or play in the snow. Sit under the stars by a campfire or watch the sunrise or sunset somewhere quiet. The advantages of this are that you can do it together, the outdoors doesn't generally charge an admission fee and kids get so much out of it physically, emotionally, mentally and intuitively.

• If you feel their zoning out is taking up too much time at the expense of other things, for example homework, then set some boundaries, but as much as possible allow for the spontaneity of this style of intuition.

• Keep them in touch with their own miracle of nature: their body. Kids who spend a lot of time daydreaming might need to be reminded to get active and do some exercise.

Visualisation: The Paint Pixies

Go out to the park or to the garden and lie in the grass. Look at the clouds scudding across the sky. Now close your eyes. Imagine all the colours in the garden have got mixed up. The grass is blue and the sky is green – it's all topsy-turvy. What has happened? You know you need to find out. Right beside you there is a secret trapdoor in the ground. Only you know where it is. You lift it up and when no-one is looking you quickly climb down the ladder that goes deep under the ground. The walls have bright glow-worms all the way down them, lighting the way, so it's not scary. When you get to the bottom you see a big hall. It's filled with lots of hardworking pixies mixing the paints for all the flowers and plants. Their job is to keep the garden looking bright and colourful. But one of the pixies has mixed up the paint and all the colours are wrong. There are pink daffodils and orange trees. Luckily you have a magic potion in your pocket that can change everything back. The silver potion sparkles in the glass bottle. With just one drop everything is perfect. The Pixies say thank you and they magically send you back to the garden. Open your eyes and look around. Are all the colours back to normal? Yes, they are...but if you look very closely, you might see the bits they forgot to paint.!

The Wonder of the Magical World

Children who are very in touch with their visual intuition will often see angelic beings, spirit guides or fairy-folk from a very young age. Talking about fairies and angels normally divides parents into three camps. The first group believe in them and love reading about them, the second think it's a complete load of rubbish and probably believe the author started off well but has now lost her marbles, while the third group are not sure what they believe but are open to learning more. It actually doesn't matter where you stand. It's not necessary for us to chant, 'I do believe in fairies!' but it is important to understand how our kids may use their intuition in relation to them.

Some children see fairies regularly, some rarely, but most children will have some contact with non-physical beings as they grow up. Often they don't realise the significance of these moments until they are older. These beings can appear as playmates or friends and offer comfort, nurturing and a sense of safety by their presence. This very prevalent form of childhood intuition, is sadly often lost by adulthood, as happened in my case:

"When I was a child I spent many hours reading about, playing with and talking to fairies. I was literally 'away with the fairies.' This was tolerated as a type of extreme imaginative play until I was around seven years old, when an uncle started to shame me for it, saying I was too old for that kind of thing. At the same time, my mother told me I should be reading about other things. Almost immediately I lost the ability to actually see fairies and to this day have never recovered it. I still remember how wondrous it was and I miss it."

We need to be very aware of how fragile a child's intuitive expression can be and how much we can impact it. It's not just fairy wings that are made of gossamer! It's ironic that children all over the world in many different cultures grow up with fairy stories and girls, especially, are encouraged to dress up as fairies and play with fairy magic. But it seems that if our kids start to genuinely believe they are real, parents can become quite concerned. Interestingly too there comes a point where children are seen to be too old to be playing with fairies and are encouraged to move on – as if magic is something we should grow out of!

Creating Magic

If your child is expressing their intuition in this way, be open to it because it's very precious. Apart from having charmed friends to play with, these fairy pals can be imparting simple wisdom to your child. It also opens up the world of the magical, and intuition is, at its heart, about magic. To be in touch with intuition is to transform the everyday into enchantment. Forgetting how to see the world in a magical way is, I believe, one of the greatest causes of adult human unhappiness. To keep a child connected to this wonderment is to immunise them against depression and cynicism.

As a parent of one of these children, you may find yourself wondering if what they're seeing is safe. You may ask yourself if it will frighten them, if they're disturbed or if they're making it up. You might worry that they could be teased about it or that they should have grown out of it by now. It's perfectly appropriate to check out what your child is experiencing, to establish if it's enriching, but it's also important not to let your fears influence them. Let the child be your guide. If they're happy then, ten times out of ten, they're doing just fine.

Living a Magical Life

• Intuition is magical, so encourage a sense of magic in your child's life. Capturing it can be as simple as playing with a puppy, going for a walk in the woods and finding a toadstool ring or seeing a rainbow or shooting star in the dark night.

• Tell children about fairies. Show them pictures and let them watch movies that tell about magical beings like Peter Pan and Tinkerbell. Explain that they can help us, whenever we ask.

• Read them stories about magic folk. Albert Einstein once said, "If you want your child to be brilliant tell them fairy tales. If you want them to be very brilliant, tell them more fairy tales." The same is true if you want them to be intuitive. So if you want them to be brilliant and intuitive you know what to do! For children, stories are the fuel that can fire up their intuitive world. As their own internal world becomes rich, so in turn does their intuition. Also, as kids read, they are creating in their heads a world of endless possibilities and it's all their choice. What a character looks like, how the scenes are. This is especially true when they listen to audio books on tapes or CDs. It's a visually creative workout.

"We need to be very aware of how fragile a child's intuitive expression can be and how much we can impact it"

• Get them to draw or make a model of what they see.

• If your child has an imaginary friend, be cool about it. Let your child share about it, or not, as they choose.

Heavenly Help for Seeing Angels

Kids see angels as often as fairies. In nearly every culture in the world there is an angelic tradition, so whether religious or not, we are generally quite comfortable with idea of celestial helpers being guardians to our children. The general consensus is that angels are universally benign and beatific –after all their very name means, 'Messenger of God'. That's a pretty impressive calling card! Children can see angels as serene, rapturous beings or in human form just like you and I. Some kids see angels around them all the time; others only come in contact with them when they are in need of help.

"I walk to school with two angels. I have to go past a rival school on the way to mine and most mornings I was being bullied. Things were being thrown at me or I was being threatened. One morning they [the angels] both just showed up. They look like sisters and like they are from another country – they don't have wings but I still know they're angels. They never say anything but they feel strong and I feel, well, stronger when they're beside me. I still get hassled but not nearly so much and I'm not scared anymore."
- Eleanor, aged 9.

The idea of our kids seeing things we can't see naturally brings up some fears accompanied by a powerful drive to protect them. The underlying question is always, 'is it safe'? And the answer is absolutely! Children often see angels when they are feeling vulnerable or alone, in trouble or fearful. However, the defining quality of angel presence is the love and peace that people feel when angels are around. And there are countless stories of children being saved by angelic intervention.

If your child regularly sees angels, I would say that you, and they, are both very fortunate. This is truly a beautiful form of intuition. Explain to them that they can ask these beings for help and guidance, that there's no limit to how much assistance they can give and that they are available all the time. If you want to give them some more detail on these heavenly hosts, head to a bookstore. There's a huge amount of great literature written about angels – who they are, how to use them, how to tell your Archangels from your Seraphims and which particular angels are best called upon in certain situations. For example, Archangel Michael is tops for protection, so he can shield you from bossy big brothers, while Uriel is best for ideas and can be called on for homework projects! The point is, if they are interested, there's heaps they can learn. Have fun with it. If you want to help your child connect visually with angels, again, bring angels into their everyday world in the form of stories or pictures.

Visualisation: Angel Encounter

Close your eyes and imagine yourself on a pair of magic roller-skates which take you to your favourite place. Wow! They go so fast! It can be the beach or your bedroom or wherever is special for you. Have a look around at all the things you love about this place. What can you see? You feel very loved and happy here. Now as you look around, you will see that someone was waiting for you to arrive. It's a very beautiful angel, kind and gentle and shining. Does he/she have wings? He/she knows all about you and you know you can trust them. They are like a special friend. If you want you can talk to them, ask them a question or share something that's been worrying you. Or you can just play with them in your special place. When you're finished they give you a pair of enchanted sunglasses. They tell you that they're invisible back in the real world but you can keep them in your pocket and whenever you need to see an angel you can pop them on. Then they sprinkle angel dust on your roller-skates so they can zoom you home at intergalactic warp speed. As you say goodbye, they let you know that you can come back any time you like.

Seeing Spirit Guides

There is one other type of non-physical being that children often see – spirit guides. But just what, or who, are they? According to Michael Newton PhD, author of 'Journey of Souls', spirit guides are 'spiritual beings who have our soul evolution as their special interest'. They may be people we have known, who have died, but still have a particular interest in taking care of us. This may be someone we have little memory of, such as a grandparent and it can even be someone we had a troublesome relationship with, while they were alive. In other cases, guides seem to be entirely spirit. There are no hard and fast rules.

Some people seem to have the same guidance all their lives, for others the guides change as they move through different life phases or as their spiritual understanding grows and they progress through their life's lessons – a kind of guide graduation. These guides have access to higher knowledge and greater wisdom than we currently do. Spirit guides can be allocated to us for one lifetime or many. Their purpose is to help us make the finest decisions and assist and protect us on our life journey. There's no limit to how many guides you can have – we all have a spirit support network. They can't interfere with our free will, but they may have a different perspective about what is our best path. As spirit guides want only love for us, all messages from them only come from the highest place of compassion. These wise beings have our best interests at heart and their guidance is free and constantly available – a kind of on-call spiritual life coaching.

When they appear to us, they often appear in archetypes such as red indians, magicians or religious figures which often says something about their nature, or about the issues that are presenting themselves in our lives. For example, one guide might appear as a Goddess, as they have powerful female energy and that may be what you need in your own life at that time. It might also refer to a past life experience.

I've also 'seen' guides as totem animals, pets or as elements of nature. They can transform at will and reveal their names or not. There really seems to be no end to how guides can present. What is a constant however is that they are there to help you navigate your life.

In my experience every child has at least one guide, with some having many. How these guides appear to the child varies enormously but it will always be in a form that they find highly sympathetic. Kids who are in touch with this form of intuitive guidance from a young age take it for granted and are usually surprised to find out that not everyone enjoys this special relationship so freely.

If your child is aware of their guides or has a lot of contact with them, encourage them to expand the association. Explain to them they can talk to them and ask for help if they need it. If you have an older child you can show them *how* to use their guides in a more precise way by taking them through this easy four-step...umm...guide!

The Guides Guide to Guidance!

1. Ask the question

• Decide what it is you really need help with – to prevent confusion work with one dilemma at a time.

• Ask your guides for assistance – be specific here. It's better to ask, 'Should I choose History over Biology at school', rather than 'What subject is best for me'?

• Write it down or say it out loud – this focus makes your request more powerful.

• Give your support team a time frame. Say, 'I need an answer within a week'.

2. Look for the answer

• This is the fun part, because guidance can come in many guises. Look for billboards that jump out at you, an advert on the radio that catches your attention, listen to what people say and notice who you meet, 'coincidentally'.

• Be alert – if you've asked for a sign, then don't miss it when it comes! If you're not sure you got it, ask for another to affirm the first.

• Sometimes the answer comes while we sleep. Pay attention to your dreams. When you go to sleep ask that you will know the answer when you wake in the morning.

• Be open minded, our guides can choose the most amusing ways to answer us, and it might not always be the answer we were expecting.

3. Check it's not wishful thinking

It can be tricky to separate guidance from our own desires so see if your answer matches the following…

• It doesn't tell you what to do because we all have free will and choice but it does point you in the right direction.

• The information is expansive, it's for everyone's benefit and good.

• It generally feels right

• It normally confirms what you knew deep down, (but maybe didn't want to admit!).

4. Review

• If you got your answer – great. Decide what you want to do with it – if you choose to, take action and make the decisions

• Try it again with another question – there's no end to the guidance!

• Play with the process, experiment and find out what works for you.

• If you didn't get a clear answer then you might need to re-frame the question or ask another. Sometimes it's just not the time for something to be known and the answer might be, 'patience'.

Finally, guides need quiet to communicate with us. For this reason they often appear in our children's dreams or in the space between waking and sleeping at end of the day. Try this simple exercise at these times.

Exercise: The Magic Friend

Imagine that just as you go to sleep a very magical person – it can be a wizard or enchanted princess or Red Indian Chief or anyone you like comes to you and takes your hand. Can you see them? What do they look like? Perhaps they might tell you their name? They are going to take you on a big adventure in your dreams. You might fly through the clouds or swim with dolphins and all the time they will be there to keep you safe. In the morning you will be able to remember all the fun you had and you'll feel great because' you had such a deep, relaxing sleep. So lie quietly now and wait for your magical guide to appear...

The Realm of Spirit

Children with this super-sense can regularly see people and even animals who have died. This can be someone they loved or knew, or they can be total strangers, but they are beings who have previously existed in a physical form.

In the movie, *The Sixth Sense* the little boy sees 'dead people'. The ghosts he sees show up with injuries they've died of and are terrifying to him. While this makes great entertainment it's not an accurate portrayal of this form of visual intuition. Children who see people who have left their body, see them as they would you or I, often not realising they are dead. Indeed, it's often not until children get older, that they realise that the people they spent time playing with and talking too, were actually no longer living. Alternatively, they might get a clear sense of how they died but there is no horror involved. In fact, the reverse is often true with the deceased having a very serene presence and the child feeling peaceful after the encounter. This is especially true if they had a strong heart connection with the person in question; perhaps a grandparent or friend. It's also common for visually intuitive kids to foresee or have a premonition of a death, either by seeing the events that cause it, or seeing a person who has not died as if they already have. While this sounds very dramatic, it's normally quite matter of fact. If a child has forewarning in this way it usually means one of two things. It's either a sign post from the universe that an accident or ill health can be averted or they are being gently prepared for what is to happen.

> *"Just after her second birthday, we enrolled Katie into swimming lessons. That's when we first heard of Haley. Katie told us she had to learn how to swim because Haley had told her she must. We were happy to hear that she had a new friend day-care and we asked if they know which child Haley was. They looked at us and smiled saying there was no one at the centre with that name. A little bit bewildered, my husband and I asked Katie who Haley was. Katie then told us that Haley had drowned when she was three and had told Katie it was important that she learn to swim. That was our first introduction to Haley."*
>
> *- Katie's mum, Lisa*

Scary Visions – Keeping your child on track

In rare instances, a child can have a negative experience, where they may feel overwhelmed by what they have seen. For example if they stay somewhere, where the previous inhabitants died in a difficult or painful way, or if they visit a scene where people have been injured or killed. Often what the child is picking up on is, the distress surrounding the incident – and this can be strong regardless of how long ago in history it happened

> *"Connor is ten now and full on with his spiritual vision but in hindsight I realise he was following spirit around the room when he was a baby – it used to scare me. When we first moved to NZ, we were in a house that must have been a hive of (energetic) activity and we later found out that a boy who had lived there, had been murdered in the reserve behind the property. Connor was upset for many nights. We moved out of the house for that reason. Since then he hasn't been so scared."*
>
> *- Connor's mum*

If your child does use their intuition in this way and feels scared or feels out of control because of what they are seeing, then you have a number of options.

• Let your child talk freely about what they are experiencing without judgement or criticism. If they are pre-language, watch for signs like repeated bad dreams, withdrawal or unexplained anxiety.

• Know for yourself and explain to them, that no spirit can ever harm your child. Let them know that communications from people who have left their body should be exclusively loving and positive.

• Explain to them that if they are picking up on someone's past pain or feel they don't like what they are seeing, that they can have it removed or they can distance themselves from it. Make it clear that the pain doesn't belong to them. Get them to imagine a magic garbage truck that can remove what has been left behind and take it to the dump! Underline that they are in control.

• Know for yourself that their fears are unfounded and can come quite naturally from their inexperience. Also be aware that fears can be learned and can be communicated explicitly or implicitly from the attitudes of their friends, family and culture. Ninety-nine times out of a hundred kids get scared in the presence of spirit because they don't know what to do or they already have the belief that it's a frightening phenomenon.

• If you think where you are living is the source of the problem, research the history of the area or property. If it's appropriate, do a simple space clearing with the child to cleanse the house of negative energy. You can re-paint, burn sage, imagine the entire house bathed in white light and release any pain that has been left behind in it. In most cases, this will solve the problem, but if it does persist, you might consider moving house.

• Discuss death openly in your family and answer any questions that your child asks honestly and directly.

• If your child has recently lost someone they loved, talk with them about it openly and sensitively. Children adopt healthy attitudes to death and dying when they are allowed to be part of the process. Despite the best intentions, keeping death hidden or secret to protect the child usually leads to confusion and fear. A sympathetic bereavement counsellor who specialises in children can be very helpful.

Plus Points — What do they get out of it?

The fact that our kids can see people who have left their bodies can bring up a tremendous amount of fear for parents. However, the reality is usually incredibly benign. The experience is almost always healing or beneficial in some way, especially if it involves someone they knew and trusted. Initially it might be hard to imagine what the benefits of our children using their intuition in this way might be, but actually they are profound and life-changing.

Firstly, it removes the fear of death, bringing the understanding that death is not the end. Secondly, if they have lost someone they loved and the child is tuning in, they are actually accessing a beautiful relationship that death cannot limit. It shows them they can continue to communicate – that love never dies. If children can get this at a young age, it will enhance the quality of their life and relationships for as long as they live.

> *"When Katie was three my grandad passed away. It was a very sad time for us all because it was so sudden. My husband, Katie and our other two children, and I made a twelve-hour trip to be with my grandma. One night when Katie was in the bath she was talking to Haley and telling her not to give Grandad a hard time because he was new. It gave me comfort to know Haley was looking after my grandad."*
> - Katie's mum, Lisa

Mini Workshop for Parents

If you find yourself very challenged about this then it's important to explore your own fears and beliefs. Very few of us are completely at peace on the subject of death! To help shed a little light on what might be blocking you, fill in the blanks...

- I believe that seeing people who have died is...
- My fears for my child are...
- My own fears around death are...

- I would prefer it if my child was…
- My own experience with this type if intuition is…

Heaven's Door Exercise

To help a child connect with a loved one or pet who has passed over.

Sit down with a grown up and a picture or a possession of the person or animal you want to connect with. Write a letter to them, saying all you want to share. It might just be, 'I miss you'. Then close your eyes and imagine you are in a beautiful room with all your favourite things – somewhere you feel very safe. You hear a quiet knock at the door, so you open it and the person or pet comes through. They are so happy to see you! You play together and if there is something that needs to be said, you can say it. When you are finished, say thank you for coming to visit and take them to the door. Let them know it's time to leave but they can come back whenever they are invited.

Auras and Chakras

Children who use visual intuition frequently see the physical body in an extra-sensory way. It's normal for them to be able to see and describe auras – the halo-like energy field that surrounds our bodies – and the chakras – the body's seven spinning energy centres – which are usually beyond the range of normal vision. Auras and chakras are part of our energetic body and are linked to our physical and emotional wellbeing. Healers use them to identify where we have weakness or dis-ease. If we are upset or ill, it will show up first in these energy fields.

> "When my daughter, Samantha, was 10 she asked me, 'What does it mean when you see colours around people'? She told me that while in her school assembly with 700 students, she could see all these colours around everyone,

including some of the teachers. Another time, I was relaxing on the couch when my younger daughter Katie told me I was all bluey purple. My first thought was, 'Don't tell me she can see auras as well'. Then my older daughter came in, in a typical pre-teen mood. I asked Katie, 'What colour is Becky?' Katie told me she was a red-orange, which made sense."
- Samantha, Katie and Becky's mum, Alison.

"The first time Thomas saw an aura he was three and I was in the shower. He walked in and said, 'Why is there purple around you?' The next time, it was when my teenage daughter was in a really angry mood and Thomas said she had bright red all around her. I didn't know what it represented for him."
- Thomas' mum, Debbie.

Kids can see chakras and auras from a very young age. This makes a lot of sense when you consider how appealing colour is to a child. Very young children are attracted to, and see the world, in terms of colours. That's why so many early childhood toys are vividly multicoloured. Like Thomas' mum, if we don't understand what our children are seeing it can be very frustrating for us and them. So it's worthwhile learning and teaching them some basics about auras and chakras. The best approach is just to give them information about it, like you would the rest of their body. So you can get them to point to their toes and their throat chakra – how cool is that!?

Rainbow Aura Chart

There can be lots of colours in someone's aura. While the colours can mean different things to different people, some shades typically represent certain qualities.

• ***Red = Anger, Change, Vitality and Power / Ambition***
Often seen around physically intuitive children.

• ***Orange = Pleasure, Sensuality, Creativity and Joy***
Can be seen around nurturing, emotionally intuitive children.

• *Yellow = Energy, Intellect, Insight and Happiness*
Common around children who are beginning to use their intuition.

• *Green = Harmony, Balance, Love, Eco-Aware*
Frequently seen around kids who are intuitive healers.

• *Blue = Inspiration, Freedom, Healing and Expression*
Signifies children who are intuitive communicators.

• *Indigo = Wisdom, Spiritual, Perception and Foresight*
Often seen around visually intuitive children.

• *Violet = Enlightenment and Higher Consciousness*
A marker for highly intuitively evolved children.

• *Pink = Childlike, Gentle, Warmth and Safety*
Usually seen around children of all ages.

• *White = Purity, Truth, Protection and Innocence*
Often seen in the auras of young souls or those who are intuitively very open.

• *Gold = Brilliance, Divine Radiance, Love and Abundance*
An indicator of profound, intuitive awareness in a child. Can also protect against negativity.
• *Black = Fear, Hate, Pain and Suffering*
This can indicate illness, stress, strong emotion, negative beliefs or the misuse of power.

Children who can see auras might also describe them as being 'out of shape', or they might say that the colours are muted and/or cloudy. These can all signify that the person's energy is compromised in some way. Teach them to clean their own aura with the imaginary, magic dust-buster that sucks up any yucky bits.

Hello Halo — How to Read an Aura

If you want to teach your child to see an aura, have fun with this simple game.

- To see them in the mind's eye — Have the child close their eyes and imagine the colours and shape around their body. Then get them to open their eyes and draw a picture of what they saw.
- To see them externally — Stand against a blank wall and have your kid stand about four metres away. Make sure the room has no bright lights. Get them to close their eyes for half a minute. Tell them to slowly open their eyes and look past you. Ask them to imagine a see-through, marshmallow-type blob around your body. Get them to say if what they see has any colours or distinguishing features. Explain that it can take a little practice, so they might have to try a few times! Let them have fun trying it out on pets, plants or friends.

Chakras for Kidz

Chakras also have colours and are associated with certain parts of the body. Here is a guide to the chakras and what they represent. You can call them by their proper names or for younger children, make up some more user-friendly titles. See my favourites in brackets!

- **Base Chakra** (*Bottom* or *Giggle Chakra*) — Red
Security, money and approval.

- **Naval Chakra** (*Belly Button Chakra*) — Orange
Fertility and sexuality.

- **Solar Plexus Chakra** (*Bulls-Eye Chakra*) —Yellow
Tied to personal power and relationships.

- **Heart Chakra** (*Love-Heart Chakra*) — Green
Giving and receiving love.

• **Throat Chakra** (*Cake-Hole Chakra*) – Blue
Communication, speaking up and creativity.

• **Third Eye Chakra** (*Cyclops Chakra*) – Indigo
Free will and clear seeing.

• **Crown Chakra** (*Prince* or *Princess Chakra*) – Violet
Higher consciousness and understanding.

Exercise Chakra Circus

Close your eyes and picture yourself standing in the middle of a giant circus tent. You are an amazing Chakra Clown dressed in all the colours of the rainbow. You throw seven coloured balls in the air. They are red, orange, yellow, green blue, indigo and violet. Can you see them? When the drum rolls you start to juggle them – you are very good at it and everyone claps. But then the balls start to juggle all by themselves in the air – it's magic. Then they stop moving and line up in order; red at the bottom, indigo at the top. They are all spinning and each one makes its own sound. Each colour has a different note, so all together they sound like a song – they are very pretty. Look at the balls spinning in the air. Are they all perfectly round? Are any spinning too fast or too slow? Do any have dark or raggedy marks on them? If so, then just imagine that they are the perfect shape and speed and they will pop back to how they should be. Pop. Pop. It makes you feel good to see them all in perfect working order. It's time to finish now, so you whistle to them to come with you out of the ring. They line up all bright and shiny, perfectly balanced one after the other and follow you out of the tent. The crowd cheer and whistle. You can play with them anytime you like.

It's clearly a huge advantage to be able to perceive auras and chakras. It means your child can see what's going on physically and emotionally for others and themselves and bring things back into balance if necessary. You might mention to them that it's wise to be prudent who they share their information with. Great Aunt Nellie might not want to know that her Base Chakra is looking a bit pale and wobbly when she drops in for tea! Likewise the school headmaster might not appreciate being told that his aura is puke green and out of shape.

This raises an important issue for children who are using their super-senses. Children are very generous with information and might not always understand when it's inappropriate to speak about what comes to them intuitively. So who can they tell? What is good intuitive etiquette? In general, a good rule of thumb is if it's not someone who lives with you or who is a good friend, check with Mum or Dad first. It's also a good idea to teach your kids that it's polite to ask someone's permission first, before you give them information. These two guidelines will keep your switched-on Gen I's out of a lot of trouble!

Who to tell?

Always tell:	*Check with Mum / Dad / Carer First:*	*Be careful about telling:*
Mum	Good friends	Strangers
Dad	Close family	Distant friends & family
Primary carer	Teachers	Neighbours you don't
Best friends	People you trust	know very well

Colour Me…Everything

To encourage the exploration of the world of auras and charkas, expose your child to colour – let them paint, play and experiment with it. Break out from the rigid gender conditioning that surrounds our kids and colour.

Let boys play with pink and girls have something that's not rosy or purple. Children, like adults, are often attracted to the colour they most need to be surrounded by in terms of healing. So as much as is practical, let them choose the hues that are on their walls and on their clothes. Show them pictures of auras and halos around angels and explain how energy is around us all, all of the time.

Star Colours

Whether your child is a fish or a twin, their astrology sign has a colour to bring them back into balance.

What colour is your kid?
• *Capricorn* – Indigo – inspires intuition, creativity, individuality and fearlessness. Wearing it can help with sleeping problems and calms nerves.
• *Sagittarius* – Blue – inspires loyalty, freedom, inventiveness. Wearing it helps with fever.
• *Libra* – Green – inspires harmony, compassion and generosity. Wearing it helps with headaches and digestion problems.
• *Leo* – Yellow – inspires optimism, confidence, good humour. Helps if your child is tired or a little sad.
• *Taurus* – Red/Orange – inspires sporty energy, vibrance, strong will. Wearing it helps if your kids are tired or cold.
• *Gemini* – Orange – inspires joy, enthusiasm, self-assurance. Wearing it will help if your child has allergies.
• *Cancer* – Yellow/Orange – Inspires independence, positivity, clarity. Wearing it will help if your children have weight problems (too little or too much)
• *Aries* – Red – Inspires honesty, strong will, forgiveness. Wearing it helps kids with poor circulation.
• *Pisces* – Red/Violet – thoughtfulness, mental strength, kindness. Wearing it helps children when they are feeling emotional.
• *Aquarius* – Violet – inspires idealism, justice, self-sacrifice. Wearing it

can help strengthen creativity.

• *Scorpio* – Blue/Green – inspires self-control, love of children, flexibility. Wearing it helps if your child has had a shock.

• *Virgo* – Yellow/Green – inspires wide horizons, sympathy, humility. Wearing it helps kids calm down.

Intuition and Energetic Protection

One of the bonuses about teaching kids about the energetic body is that we can introduce to them the idea that other people's energy can sometimes get mixed up with our own, especially if they are feeling bad or angry. Explain to them that sometimes our auras can get a bit sticky if we haven't cleaned them for a time and they can pick up other people's slimy energy. Tell them that they can keep their aura spick and span by closing their eyes and imagining it having a shower of white light – just like they do in the bathroom with water. It only takes a minute, then it's done. If only it was so easy to clean their bedrooms!

Vivid Intuitive Dreams

Visually intuitive kids often have startlingly intricate night-time dreams with complete dream recall when they wake. Dreams are a complex form of communication from our subconscious that can be profoundly useful with careful interpretation. What singles out visually intuitive dreams is that they often become reality. Children who recognise a situation unfolding in the way they dreamt it describe the experience as being similar to the sensation of deja vu – they know they have been there before. The relationship between when the dream occurs and when it manifests in the waking world can appear quite random. It can happen the next day or the next year, but regardless of the timing, the dream echo will be easily remembered.

"I have dreams. Sometimes they're showing me what's going to happen when I'm older."
- Ethan Stevens, aged nine and a half.

Everyone, including children, dreams every night – whether they remember it or not – so it's one of the most highly accessible forms of intuition you can introduce to your kids. Dreams can also be incredible tools for divination – getting wise advice – and they're on our doorstep so to speak, so it's worth taking advantage of them. There are a couple of things to watch out for, however.

Strong intuitive dreams can be as unsettling for children as they are for adults. Dreams by their nature have a distorted or surreal feel, and symbolic and predictive dreams may be even more vivid. They can make for a restless night and leave a child a little emotionally 'hung-over' the next day. The line between dream and real life can feel a little blurred.

If your child is having strong dreams then it's essential to uncover why. First, make the distinction between super-sight dreams and nightmares. All children have nightmares occasionally but if night terrors are repetitive – happening every week or so – with your child waking distressed or fearful about going to bed, then you need to consult a health professional. These dreams are normally reflective of something that is upsetting your child in their waking life.

Strong intuitive dreams, while sometimes unsettling, can also feel euphoric or deeply peaceful. They can be about past lives or the future. Children usually innately know that the intuitive dream they had was different, or stood out from their run-of-the-mill dreams. Intuitive dreams are very powerful. In some cases, children will remember them for years.

However they affect your child, it's worthwhile taking the time to get them clear on what they've 'seen' while asleep.

"I dreamt I'm going to be a writer. I had a giant pen and I was giggling in the dream. When I woke up, I told everyone that telling stories is what my job will be."
- Holly, aged seven.

If you want to support your child in this type of intuition then there are lots of practical things you can do:

- Invite them to talk about their dreams and how they feel about them.
- Encourage your child to keep a dream journal. Get them to write and draw what they've dreamt.
- Get hold of a good book on dream imagery, read up about it and use it for reference. Many apparently confusing or troublesome dreams can be easily explained this way and the emotional impact defused.
- Check in periodically on how their dream world is affecting them. Do they seem tired or rested? Are they happy or wary about going to bed?
- Explain that a dream can be like a weather forecast from the future, telling us what's on its way, but stress that not all dreams come true. Over time they'll get a feel for the difference. Also reassure your child that just because they dreamt it, it doesn't mean they somehow made it happen. This is particularly important if they dream about death.
- Show your child that dreams can carry secret messages – messages that can teach them things they need to know, either about what will happen or what is happening in their lives. Just bringing this knowledge into awareness means they will look at their dreams differently.
- If your child wakes remembering a bad dream, walk them through it again and have them change the end so it has a good outcome. 'Dream re-framing' in this way is a very potent tool and reminds the child that they are in control of their dream world and who shows up there.

Before your child goes to sleep, you can set things up to help them connect with pleasant intuitive dreams:

- Read magical bedtime stories
- Let them fall asleep listening to soothing music
- If they have a problem, suggest to them that the answer might come to them gently while they sleep.
- If they've been dreaming a lot, tell them to turn off the dream machine and have a peaceful night or to watch their dreams like they would a football match – at a distance in the stand.

The Past

Kids will often see details about places and people that once existed that they could not have known about. This can include information about past lives – their own and others' – and historic events. This can happen spontaneously but is usually triggered by visiting or reading about, locations that resonate with them. Or it can be after watching a movie, learning about a period of history, a past way of life or a famous person from the past. This can show itself in a number of ways, from the child who is completely fascinated with a certain time in history and works to have an encyclopaedic knowledge of that period to the kid that points out, while you are walking around an old castle that the library was down the hall, not here, as it says on the wall plaque!

This type of intuition can be spine-tingling because children often link through time with themselves in past lives or with other children they may or may not have known. In the same way that children are drawn to each other in life there seems to be a specific energy connection for little people across death too.

"When Jaye, my daughter, was 12 she read incessantly about the Holocaust. She was obsessed with the Jews and what happened to them in the concentration camps of Europe during WW2. Every TV program or children's book that even touched on the subject would attract her like a magnet. To be honest, I felt her interest was pretty morbid and a little unhealthy but I didn't stop her. She explained matter-of-factly that she remembered this happening to her and that she'd died in the gas chambers, aged four. She said that she was reading to find out what happened afterwards to the people she loved. It sounds bizarre, but it made perfect sense that she was searching for closure in this life for what had happened in the last – finding an explanation, for what, at the time, must have been beyond reason. Interestingly Jaye has also had an interest in all things Polish – the language, the people and the food – even although we have no links to Poland. Later she visited Warsaw, the capital, on a school trip. While staying there she went exploring. With absolutely no prior knowledge of the city she went, as we later discovered, straight to the area that had been the Jewish Ghetto – it was not marked on any map and the original buildings have all been demolished. She said the whole time she was walking around the

boundary, all she could think of was that she needed to 'find home'."
- Jaye's dad, Martin.

While Jaye's story shows a very strong past life connection, every child will reveal past life resonances if you look for them.

"My son Callan, 8, has always had two very interesting personality traits. He is remarkably kind to younger children — an attribute that every teacher he's had has commented on. He also has very expensive tastes! Even at five, he had an eye for quality and is drawn to grand houses and luxury of all kinds. I wasn't surprised then, when a healer who didn't know me or my son told me in passing that Callan had lived as a very wealthy man, probably royalty, and had devoted a great deal of his money and time to helping street children. She said in this lifetime, Callan's soul contract was about learning that he couldn't always be first — the King of the Castle, if you like. I might add that this is very important to him."   *(Author)*

Apart from a budding career as a historian, you might well wonder what relevance this type of intuition could have for your child. Where's the value in being able to intuit the past? The answer is in the present. We are the sum of where and who we have been. According to the law of Karma, we come back to get right, the things we didn't manage to get right in a past life. How much more helpful would it be if we could access detailed information about this for ourselves and others?! If we knew what issues we had to address, we could get them out the way a lot faster. These children are using their gifts to reveal and heal the past, and move on to a future free from what has gone before. I also believe that what we heal in the present can change the past — so these kids are literally re-writing karma and becoming masters and mistresses of their own destiny. Impressive, isn't it?

Intuition that involves past lives can ask us to suspend a great deal of cynicism. Even although I've personally had quite a few astonishing past life memories and experiences and spoken to children who've had many more, it's frankly still a big thing to get your head around. Even if you are not really a believer it's important that you take your child seriously when they are describing these kinds of experiences to you. Even if you struggle with the idea that we may have lived before, your child needs to feel that you are listening and that you understand.

To encourage your child to connect with this type of intuition, you need to bring history alive. Visit historic houses, monuments and places. Go to museums and learn about past cultures and people. Wherever possible, indulge your child's interest in any particular time or place in history. Encourage them to write stories, dress up or play imaginative games, where they are a hero or heroine from a time past. This is great fun and can be very educational too.

Intuition and the Perception of Time

Regardless of whether your child can see the past or the future, when they are using their intuition they may experience fluidity around the conventional notion of time. Indeed intuition will often take them outside time. I'm not talking here about how children lose time, when they are absorbed in something they love; rather this is when the normal boundaries around time seem to stretch or wobble. Their experience of this can vary. Time can be felt to stand still or it can just completely stop existing. They will feel 'outside' of time. While sometimes disorientating, this is usually a very pleasurable sensation and is important. Children can start to understand that time is a construct and intuition does not always work within it. Actually, intuition regularly transcends time and space as the experience I had as a young teenager highlights:

"I was waiting for a train on a summer's evening. It was due in a few minutes and there was no-one else on the platform and I was enjoying the space. All at once I experienced a shift in the scene around me. The only way I can describe it was as if I had suddenly become an observer of what was happening and someone had hit a pause button. Everything stood still, the air, the sounds, there was only complete peace, inside and out. It was so beautiful I never wanted it to end. When the train came, I felt I had been there all day. Time had stretched endlessly between the minutes."

Exercise: The Magic Book of You

Close your eyes and imagine that you are standing in an enchanted library in front of a giant colour book. On the cover is your name. This is your special book of you. When you open it, you can see pictures from your life – all your family and friends, everywhere you have been and all the good times you've had. The pictures move like mini video clips. It's great to look at. And the amazing thing about this book is that it has pictures of all the lives you have ever lived – not just this one. So flick back a few pages and see what your life before this one was like. Are you boy or a girl? What are you wearing? What country are you living in? Can you see the house you lived in? Is there anyone you recognize? When you've finished looking you can turn to the very last page in the book. There's something written just for you. Can you see it? It tells you why you are here this time and what you have come to learn and give. What does it say? Can you tell? Don't worry if you can't make it out yet. You can come back and have a look anytime you like.

The Future

Accurately seeing the future is perhaps one of the most sensational things that Gen I children can do.

"Mia has a game that she plays whenever we are going somewhere new on holiday. She draws a picture of the place we are going to stay in by imagining what it will look like. In each case she's never been there before and hasn't even seen pictures of our destination. They are accurate, to the smallest of details – even the door colour! The first time she did it, my husband and I were so gob-smacked I took photos and put them up against her drawing and showed all our friends. We still can't fathom how she does it but it's great fun for her."

- Lauren, mum of Mia, aged 9

For some children doing what Mia does is an everyday event. Unlike seeing the past, the appeal of being able to see the future is enticing for all of us. Who doesn't want to know what the future holds sometimes? For this reason, humans have been fascinated for thousands of years by the possibility that some have an ability to accurately predict the future. Tools of divination like Runes and the Tarot, which are very ancient, have all come from a desire to harness this potential. But seeing the future still has an aroma of fortune-telling – a neat trick practised by gypsies with crystal balls. So how is it possible for our children to get images of the future internally? Well, firstly we need to re-evaluate how we see time. There is a brilliant moment in the docu-movie on Quantum physics, *What the Bleep Do We Know*, when one of the scientists comments that it's interesting we think it's normal to see into the past but not into the future." This is a very good point. We think of time as linear but it's possible and likely, that in actual fact past, present and future are all happening simultaneously. If this is true then anyone who has the super-sense to tune into this parallel energy can 'view' the future because it's not really the future, it's now.

Also, it's my belief that our futures are not fixed; they change with every decision we make – a bit like a computer game. Or as William Blake so succinctly put it, "There is no fate but that we make". If we follow that line of thought then it is clear that we create our reality depending on our choices, and so whatever we focus on, comes into being. The more energy we are directing at an outcome the more certain that outcome becomes. Children who are sensitive to energy can tap into this flow and see where it's leading. They can predict the most likely result given the intention of the person, even if that intention is not at a conscious level. As we begin to understand our universe in energetic terms we can see that what used to be thought of as sorcery, is in fact universal law in action. The point is we need to demystify what is an incredibly useful intuitive tool, so our kids can use it like they do logarithms.

" I've always been able to see the future for as long as I can remember – I don't even think of it as strange. I actually get more spooked when I miss something that I think I should've picked up. I don't know how people live without being able to do it. For me it would be like being deaf or blind. The biggest thing I've seen? I was watching a plane taking off over the city and I 'saw' it crash. I

thought, 'Why am I seeing that? That's not gonna happen, I'm just imagining some drama 'cos I'm bored.' Just then, there was a loud bang, and the aircraft kinda dropped a little in the sky, turned round and went back to land. I was really scared. Later I heard on the news it had been an emergency...some engine problem, no-one was hurt. That was weird — it was like, yeah I can really do this stuff...I should respect it more."
- Ella, aged 12.

Teaching your kids to respect their intuition and not take it for granted is always good. If your child frequently sees what's to come, explain that knowing the future is useful, but being happy in the present is the greatest gift. Kids who have this super-sense can find it hard to live with uncertainty, especially as they get older. When you regularly get windows into what's pending, it can be frustrating when you can't 'see' everything that's coming, when you really want to. For example, I might 'see' there's a fabulous opportunity headed my way but I might not be able to make out what that is.

Intuiting the future can be elusive and we don't always get the full picture. You will be doing your child a big service if you explain to them that not everything is going to be revealed to them about the days ahead. Make them realise also that their lives would be meaningless if they could intuit the entire outcome anyway. If they can learn acceptance, let go of trying to control what's to come and understand that sometimes it really is better not to know, they'll be able to use this super-sense with maturity. Show them that working out the gaps between what they 'see' and what pans out is the fun part! Finally — and this is the most important of all — teach them that regardless of what they see there's always free will and choice involved. A certain situation might be a given but how they respond to it is entirely up to them — like the time I saw that my bag was going to be stolen at school. It was still taken but I had emptied it of all my prized possessions first!

Intuition Hot Spot: View from the top

Why can some children see some phenomena and not others? Well, some kids just have aptitude in particular areas. But there is another factor, and that is, you can see what you believe is possible. The biggest barriers to any type of intuition are fear, prejudice and negative beliefs. If your child believes they can do something and no-one has told them they can't or it's bad, then sooner or later they will be able to do it. If they are scared or concerned about it, then it's going to be that much harder. Intuitive vision is always narrowed by fear. So, if you want to encourage your child's ability to see the future in this way then start by telling them it's possible.

Exercise: Back to the Future

Close your eyes and imagine you are sitting in a movie theatre. The movie is about to start and it's dark in the cinema. The curtains draw back and you push a button so the projector starts to shine it's light on the screen. The movie is about your life, not now, but sometime in the future. Can you see yourself? How old are you? Where are you? What's happening in the movie? Watch it play on the screen. If you want you can get it to rewind and watch it again or play it slightly differently this time. See what feels best for you. When you are finished, switch of the projector. The movie will come to an end and you can open your eyes. If you want to know how something is going to turn out, you can come back to the movie theatre and watch the movie of your life any time you like.

Seeing Signs and Symbols

Most children who use visual intuition will get their information to some degree in the form of symbols or signs. Of all forms of visual intuition this can be the hardest to decipher because it's the child who has to work out what their meaning is — this can't be taught. The best advice for parents here is to let meaning emerge over time and accept that there is something worthwhile here even if it's not clear immediately.

Intuitive Vision: Guided Visualisation

Close your eyes. Now imagine you are in a garden, lying on the grass. Suddenly the earth starts to shake and quake and a huge red digging machine bursts out of the earth next to you. In it is a very cranky gnome. His white beard has got sticks and roots in it. He's taken the wrong turn and is lost. He explains he needs to go down deep in the centre of the earth and asks if you want to come along. You say yes and jump on board. The machine turns around and starts to sink into the soil at super-fast speed. You hang on as you go deeper and deeper. It's very dark, there are no lights here and you can't see a thing. Finally the digger stops and you get out into a huge black cave. It's so dark you can't see your own hands. The gnome laughs as you stumble about. Then he puts his hand in his pocket and pulls something out. He opens his hand and out floats a bright shining white ball of light. Immediately the whole cave is lit up. You can see every nook and cranny. Everywhere there are gnomes digging or sifting through the earth and in the middle is a ginormous pile of crystals of all different sizes and colours – it's a giant gnome mine! The floating light shines brighter still and you realise you can see through the walls of the cave, through the earth, past the buried dinosaur bones up, up through the ground and to the sky. You can see deep into space without end. You can see everything! The gnome explains that the light is actually a star that fell from the heavens and when it's on you can see everything there is to see. He says the gnomes use it to find the crystals, which are so precious. He bends down and with his stumpy fingers he picks up a twinkling clear crystal on the ground. He hands it to you and tells you that it will always help you to see everything clearly. He asks you to close your eyes, everything goes dark and when you open them you are back in your room. Wow, that was quick! Now if you like you can draw a picture or play a game of what it's like to be able to see everything.

Chapter 4
Intuitive Audio

Intuitive Audio is the hearing super-sense. This chapter investigates the different ways that 'Super Hearing' can manifest in our children.

The Inner Voice

In its simplest form, Intuitive Audio is a type of intuition we have all experienced at some point. The still, small voice within us that speaks enormous wisdom has long been recognised and written about in different cultures across many centuries. We all know about it – even if we don't always pay attention to it! You may have heard it as a whisper in a quiet moment, suggesting that you take one job over another or sometimes it can be more insistent, urging you to stop the car or leave the highway and you find out later that day that there was a smash further ahead just at that time.

Children hear this voice in the same way as adults but because they generally have less resistance, they can hear it more intensely and more often. They will describe it as being like a thought inside their head but more distinct. Alternatively, they might say it's as if someone has spoken out loud in the room but only they seemed to notice it. This clarity can be so profound that Gen I's may feel as if they can actually hear themselves talking out loud. As a child, this type of intuition saved my life:

"When I was eleven, I was playing at the park with friends – there were no adults around. The others were a little distance away when a man came up to me and said he had lollies in his car and if I would like to come with him and get in the car I could have them. Of course I knew not to go with strangers but there's always part of a child that feels they should do what an adult asks. Suddenly, all of my intuition was shouting danger to me and in my ears I heard a rushing and a voice shouting, 'Run, Run, RUN!' I sprinted and picked up my bike and raced for my life, shouting at the others to scatter too. He tried to grab me but I was too fast and I got away. The police told me I had been very lucky. But I knew then, as I do now, that luck had nothing to do with it. My intuition had saved me. I know if I hadn't run, I wouldn't be here today."

Of all the forms of intuition, this one is the most commonly accessed when we are in danger because it's so immediate. The beauty of this type of intuition is, it's direct guidance. If you hear someone shouting at you in your head, you take notice! If you want your kids to be able to do this, you need to first explain about the inner voice – what it is and how it works. You might find they already know what you're talking about. Then give them the chance to practice with it. Kids will automatically use their intuition when they have to make a choice. Let them experiment with it by giving them some decisions to make – and explain to them how they can listen for the voice to help them. You can be explicit about it and say, 'What is your inner voice saying now?'

For kids who use this super-sense a lot, this voice plays constantly and they can hear it as clear as you can hear the radio. If it gets to be too much for them, explain that they can turn down the volume, just as they would on a stereo. It's also a good idea to work with them on the subtle difference between the inner voice and the ego. If your eight-year-old tells you that they've just heard they should have a third helping of ice-cream, you know they might need a bit of guidance! As a general guideline, the inner voice should always lead to us being more of who we are, whether emotionally, physically, mentally and intuitively.

Nurture it! Here's how you can help:
• Sing songs with them. Let them open their own voice with singing and chanting. Singing and music in all forms is tremendously important because it's like a lightning rod to our children's emotions and souls.
• Read with them out loud, especially poetry, rhymes and stories that play with sounds. Most traditional nursery rhymes are fantastic for this.
• Teach your child to really listen to what people are saying to them. Bring their awareness to the different timbre of voices and accents that we hear every day. If someone is talking to them and they are distracted, remind them to put on their giant Goblin listening ears!
• Let them play with a tape recorder and hear their own voice recording.

Intuition Hot Spot: Distant Voices

Often if children start describing that they can hear voices, parents and carers become very concerned. This is largely because of the huge association that hearing voices in your head has with mental illness. There is the fear that either the child is developing Schizophrenia, or he or she is disturbed, especially if the voices continue or become overwhelming. There are very clear distinctions between a child with super-audio skills and a child who needs help. If your child hears voices, they should be positive and loving and leave your child feeling peaceful. The voices may warn of danger but should not frighten your child. The child should feel the voices can be trusted and if they do feel overwhelmed, it should only be occasionally and in a way that is easily dealt with. If voices or sounds are negative, judgmental, unloving or causing anxiety, they are coming from the child's own fears and it's advisable to seek appropriate counselling or a medical opinion.

Children who are listening in to other voices, can usually be seen to be tuning in. They might look away or hold their head to one side when you are talking to them or seem distracted or absent, or look as if they are listening to something else. Children who use this super-sense can find it difficult to concentrate because they are literally listening to two or more people at the

same time. Even now, I still find it hard to pay attention to information that's coming through when I'm having a conversation. This is particularly true when my guides really want my attention and start to shout! So be patient with your audio intuitive child.

Exercise: Shhhhh...

Let your child lie in a quiet space and listen to, and describe everything outside and inside themselves that they can hear. This is a very powerful little exercise so it doesn't need to take more than a few minutes.

Hearing Angels, Spirit Guides & Non-Physical Beings

Children who use their intuition in this way may also hear the voices of angels, spirit guides and other beings not in physical form. Interestingly, children have no problem differentiating between their own voice and the voices of these other beings. They can easily recognise the voices as being other than their own. If you ask them to describe why, they will quickly pinpoint that the voice is deeper, of a different gender, or sounds older or younger or even non-human. However they understand the difference, they're normally clear about the separation even if they are not sure of the source of the voice. In many cases your child will know they are hearing the words or communication from an angel, or from God, or from a special friend or pet or from aliens in space! Audio intuition from angels and guides tends to be more consistent than visual intuition, with children often hearing the same beings over a long period of time. My guess is that's because it would be disorientating and confusing to hear too many different voices in a short period. Similarly to visual intuition, kids might 'hear' people or characters, in a form they are comfortable with – for me it was Jesus but it can also be Harry Potter. Obviously I didn't actually know what Jesus sounded like and originally he probably spoke in Aramaic, which I certainly didn't. The point is that I knew it was Jesus I was hearing.

> *"Sophie has long conversations with the angels. She goes somewhere quiet and chats to them, she talks like she would to a friend, then puts her head to the side when she's listening to them. When she's doing this it's very hard to distract her and she's very dreamy during and afterwards – it relaxes her. I'm not sure what they talk about – she just seems to like to hang with them."*
> - Sophie's mum, Tyra

Children may also experience communication with these beings using sounds that are beyond words or in a form of language they don't recognise but even so, they understand what is being said. No translation is necessary. If there is confusion and children don't understand what they are hearing, they make believe they have a magic translator button in their ear, which makes it all clear.

You can introduce your child to the concept of external guidance at any age. Explain to them about angels and guides and explain to them how they can ask for help or the answer to any question. Let them know that heavenly reassurance and support is available in this way, at any time they choose. Switch on your child's intuitive hearing by letting them listen creatively. There are lots of great magical stories on audio CD or tape for kids – try your local library or a good bookstore. Have a selection handy in the car or at bedtime as an alternative to reading with them.

Exercise: Angel Dreaming

Close your eyes and imagine that you are sitting high in the sky on a cloud. You can hear the wind blow and the noise of the cloud creaking as it rocks in the breeze. In the distance you can hear a big swishing noise and bells chiming. It's the sound of an angel/fairy/guide coming your way, surfing in on a cloud. Wow! I didn't know they could do that, did you? Oops, she overshot the cloud. It's okay, she's turned around and come and landed beside you. Can you hear the rustle of their golden gown? You sit quietly together watching the Earth far down below. The angel tells you that everything in the world has a sound, even rainbows and the moon. She gives you a magic silver shell and says that whenever you want to hear her you should hold the shell to your ear. She asks you if you want to ask her anything. Do you? If you do, she answers you. Then she flies off with a big swoosh of her wings. When you're ready, you slide back down a rainbow to Earth. As you zoom down, all the colours hum in harmony. You can catch a passing cloud anytime you like.

Voices of Loved Ones or Strangers Who Have Died

Intuitive hearing also extends sometimes to loved ones or strangers who have died. This is very common and younger children especially often think nothing of it. For them it's just an extension of talking to people 'in heaven'. The difference is that they get an answer.

"About six months after my Grandfather died, our family took a camping trip to scatter his ashes. Grandad's sister came with us to say goodbye to Grandad. She had also lost her husband nearly two years beforehand. On the day we scattered Grandad's ashes it was a sad event. But Katie was up to her usual antics. She walked up to Aunty Lily and asked, 'Do you know an Uncle Will?' Surprised, Aunty Lily answered, 'Yes I do, he was my husband.' Katie

then pointed to the tent Aunty Lily was sleeping in and said, 'Uncle Will says hello and he loves you.' This startled Aunty Lily, and tears welled in her eyes. Afterwards she said, 'I often think he's around but it's wonderful to know he really is.'"

- Katie's mum, Lisa

Katie's story is a beautiful example of why this form of intuition is so precious. The opportunity to stay connected with a person or pet who they cared about, or to connect someone else with someone they loved, plus the knowledge that there's more to us than just the physical body is worth so much. And don't worry that death might scare them. Children are naturally fascinated by it. Whatever your religious orientation, at some point children, usually around the age of three, will ask you about where we go after we die.

Essentially I don't think it matters how you describe it, as long as the imagery is deeply reassuring and loving. What young children need to know, is that wherever they end up they will be looked after and be happy. For older kids you can admit you don't actually know for sure, but tell them what you hope for and get them to imagine how they would like the after-life to be. Either way, take time with them to talk to loved ones in 'heaven' and let them have conversations with those they have loved and lost.

If your child uses this super-sense easily and they are upset by what they are hearing or feel overwhelmed, get them to put on some 'enchanted headphones'. Explain that they work to keep out voices we don't like but let in the ones we do. Again, try and be open about death – it's one of our greatest teachers. If a death occurs in your family or community, use it as an opportunity for learning and let your child attend the funeral if possible.

Have a death celebration where you have a party and remember all the great things about that person or pet's life. Raise your kids' awareness about different cultures' attitudes to death and the after-life, past and present. I find a visit to the Egyptian Mummy section of my local museum a great starting point for this!

Exercise: The Magic Phone

Close your eyes and imagine you have a magic mobile phone in your hand. It can dial straight through to heaven! And you can hear really clearly. Is there someone you would like to talk to? Push the silver button and let it ring. The person you want to speak to will answer. Can you hear them? Talk to them now and let them answer. You can chat for as long as you like – it's always a cheap rate to heaven! When you're finished, say goodbye and hang up. Remember to put the phone somewhere safe. You can dial up anytime you like.

Hearing People Who Are Not Present

Children might also hear what's being said even if the people who are speaking are not actually present – they could be in the next room or in another state altogether and still be energetically heard.

Intuitive listening also extends to hearing what is not spoken out loud. Some kids can pick up internal dialogue just as easily as we hear conversation. Commonly they might respond to family or friends who are present but who are not actually talking. These kids are listening to what is being thought rather than said. Children who do this can find it a little disconcerting – it can take them some time to work out how to distinguish between what they are hearing internally and externally. Reassure them that they are actually hearing what they think they are, and let them know that distance is no barrier to keeping in touch with someone. If they do intuitively eavesdrop on what people are thinking, teach them how to use that information if it's useful to them, but also to respect the person's privacy. A great lesson for all budding intuitives! This super-sense is frequently used by mothers around their children and in crisis situations. People who find themselves in dire need can spontaneously transmit emergency, intuitive messages to those close to them. Ask your child to always let you know if they receive an energetic SOS from someone and also let them know that they can send messages for help themselves if they need to.

"I 'hear' my boys a lot. If they're away somewhere playing I will 'hear' them tell me they've had enough and want me to go pick them up. If I ignore it, I get this intuitive nagging, accompanied by a growing feeling of tension over the energetic airwaves until I go get them. I also 'hear' the boys while they sleep — it's easy to tune into them then. If they are restless I can 'hear' what's bothering them."
- Roula, mum of Peter and Troy

Exercise: The Amazing Listening Bug

Close your eyes and imagine that you have a small box in your hands. In it is a bug. It's not just any bug, it's an amazing listening bug. It's all different colours like a fire opal and when you hold it in your hand you can hear what people are thinking – no matter how far away they are. Do you have a friend or grandparent who lives a long way away? Or maybe in the next street? Well, with this bug you can hear them like they are in this room. So, get it out of the box and hold it in your hand. Have you got it? Be careful not to squash it! Good. So listen in – what are they saying? You can send messages with this bug too so if you want them to hear something you just think it and off it will go, like a magic SMS message. When you are finished, you can put the bug back in the box.

Hearing the Animal Kingdom

Some children with this intuitive audio super-sense have the ability to listen to and understand pets' 'thoughts' and to hear wildlife that is a long distance away or hiding amongst trees and not visible to the naked eye.

I met an extraordinary young man, Steve, on Safari in the Northern Territory in Australia. Steve had a super-sense gift with animals, which had been honed due to the large amount of time he'd spent with Aboriginal trackers living in the desert. Indigenous people are natural intuitives and they had shown him how to tune in his senses to be aware of wildlife. His talents were awesome. He picked out and later caught, a frill-necked lizard that was perfectly camouflaged against a tree two hundred metres back from the road as we drove past at 80 kilometres an hour. It was so astonishing that even after I saw him do it I thought he must have nailed the lizard to the bark earlier! But his most stunning ability was hearing animals that we were oblivious to. He would just turn around and pick some critter out of a hole while we were standing deafly by. One day as we were trekking he answered a question I had quietly asked of a friend while we were walking over half a kilometre behind. I asked him how he knew what I had said and he blushed and said that he had overhead our conversation. His hearing super-sense made him a magician in that wilderness and what was remarkable was that even being in his presence made my sensitivity to hearing the wildlife increase exponentially.

This phenomenon of increasing your intuition just by being close to someone who is using theirs strongly is worth checking out. The old adage that, 'We don't become like the people we are with, we actually become them' is true. If you want your kids' intuition to increase then increase your own and hang out with people who are doing the same. This is especially useful for parents who have one child who is more intuitively switched on than their brother or sister. Don't be concerned if one child is very interested while another is not. Intuition does flow through by a kind of energetic osmosis. If you work with one child, everyone benefits.

If you've got a child who uses their audio intuition like Steve does, encourage it every way you can. It can open the door to a wealth of career opportunities when they are older. World famous animal activists like Frenchman Jacques Cousteau, English Naturalist Gerald Durrell and Australian Steve Irwin had an intuitive passion for animals from childhood. And we need people on the planet who have a powerful empathy with animals – the future of the world and our survival depend on it. We must learn to work with the animals not against them. And who better than our mini Dr Dolittles? Kids who use their super-senses in this way are also in touch with the instinctual part of themselves – after all we're animals too! Instinct is a lower, more limited form of intuition, but it's still useful to be connected with it.

Children who have this strong intuitive connection with animals can sometimes feel more comfortable with them than with people. Make sure they're building relationships with their own species too! Also, be sure to pay attention if they feel a pet is sick or in distress.

Animal Magic

This is a fun, fast way to open up kids to their intuition because children usually have a natural affinity with animals. If they already have a close relationship with a furry or feathered friend, that's ideal. They're probably already communicating intuitively anyway but just haven't thought about what they do. All you have to do is bring their awareness to it. If they're not around a special pet, have them tune into an animal they know and trust. Get them to be quiet with the animal, touch it and see if they can 'hear' what it's are thinking. Also some members of the animal kingdom seem to connect us with our intuition faster than others. Swimming with dolphins and getting close up with whales, personally and with my boys, has been a profound and mystical experience on every occasion. I always come away with a sense of deep peace and clarity on issues in my life.

So whenever you can, let them have a wildlife encounter. Talk to them about sound in nature, echoes and how animals hear things that we can't. Get them out into it and teach them to recognise the sounds of the natural world. Draw their attention to the outside world of sound and vibration, let them be still and listen to the wind in the trees, or the waves. Let them keep a pet or regularly connect with animals. Help them learn about the animal kingdom and gain a deep respect for the miracle that our biosphere is.

Exercise: Totem Animal

Close your eyes and choose your favourite bird, insect or animal – it can be a mythical, magical animal like a Griffin or Centaur if you like. Listen to the sounds it makes and all the noises of its natural habitat (where it lives). Now imagine that you're also an animal, just like them, – playing together in the wild. What does it feel like? How do you move? What noises can you make? What does this animal think? You can go on an adventure together. Imagine exploring places that only the animals could know about. What is it like? When you come back, your animal friend might have something to tell you – secret animal business that only you should know. What do they say? It's time to come back now but remember if ever you need to, you can call on that animal's wisdom and be like them. So you can be strong like a bear or fast like a leopard, or clever like a snake! When you open your eyes you can draw a picture of your adventure if you like.

Affinity for Music and Sounds

Some children have an extra-sensory ear for music and sound. For them music is heard like a language or a mathematical pattern. In fact, they may hear with such clarity, that they 'see' it unfolding at the same time. Often they are prodigiously gifted either in playing an instrument, singing or in writing music. Music will have a strong effect on these children, which is impossible to ignore. Classically, this form of intuition shows from a very young age and can be very intense, because sound is around us all the time and we can hear it from when we are in the womb. They might also hear sounds in a heightened way, experiencing them with an immense depth and range and able to pick up every auditory nuance. Children who are this sensitive to vibrations can usually hear sound as energetic waves. Everything has a vibration and everything affects us. Like a sacred church or a beautiful home – we feel it.

"*Lizzie writes music. She's eight. She will sit down and just pour it out on the paper, complete, like she's emptying out her head. She often does it after she's been upset — it's like an emotional release. I'm not into the whole new age thing but Lizzie describes it as channelling — like she's pulling it from somewhere outside of herself and after watching her I'd have to agree this is exactly what she's doing.*"
   - *Lizzie's mum, Rita.*

Intuitive Hot Spot: What is Channelling?

Not actually something you do with the TV remote control! Channelling is the ability to receive and communicate ideas, creative inspiration or messages. This information is usually from non-physical beings, like God, Angels and Spirit Guides or simply from the universal creative source. Channelling has had a bad rap and is popularly associated with possession by an entity that somehow takes you over. However, it's not really like that — that image comes from watching too many bad horror movies! As mentioned before it's uncommon for children to channel in this way. However there are other forms of channelling, which children, and in fact all of us, can do. Channelling is simply connecting with something larger than your own awareness, so that you can bring through information. You can do it while sitting and typing at the computer — artists often channel art-work or music. Channelling is basically bringing through universal wisdom and it's available to everyone. Channelling, like all forms of intuition, is not something to be fearful of, but it's something that needs to be learned and treated with respect, like any creative endeavour.

Nurture it! Here's how you can help stimulate your kids' musical intuition:

• Create a musical world. Let your children listen to as much music as possible. Choose a wide variety of styles; classical to pop to nursery rhymes. Avoid contemporary music that has adult themes in the lyrics. Songs have immense power to influence mood – who hasn't been triggered emotionally by a piece of music? Children need to hear music that makes them feel good. Take them to kid-friendly music concerts and musical theatre.

• Have a game in the car where they listen to different pieces of music – jazz, classical, choral, dance and get them to describe how that music makes them feel and what they feel it might be about. Does the sound conjure up a picture, for example a storm or a celebration?

• Give them the experience of making sound with simple musical and percussion instruments, like a harmonica or tambourine.

• Get them into drumming. Drumming connects children with ancient rhythms and sounds. Beating one or dancing to its sounds is a gateway to intuition.

• Introduce them to the miracle of sound. Teach them how sound travels through space like a wave and what brilliant instruments our ears are.

• Play the vibrational sounds of crystal healing bowls (you can order them on CD) to relax hyperactive children. The crystal bowl music emits a very pure beautiful healing energy field. Each bowl has a particular note – they are cut and polished and tuned to pitch perfect and balance a different part of the body. The vibration will open your child to clear guidance and they will literally be bathing in positive vibrations.

If your child is already very intuitively sensitive to sound and music, then honour the link between sound, music and their emotions and be strategic about what and when you play music around them. Classical music at bedtime and as children go off to sleep is incredibly soothing. Background music can really help a child settle when they are playing or eating a meal. Louder action music can help them let off steam.

Give them quiet time – create a vacuum of silent peace once a day. And be careful of taking them into high decibel areas like rock concerts and dance parties. They can be overcome by the onslaught to their ears.

Deepening this form of intuition in our kids is, I think, one of the biggest prizes in the super-sense box of gifts. In his book, 'Journey of Souls', Michael Newton describes the presence of God as a sound – a vibration of love. Music has always been a bridge between our humanity and ecstatic experience – something which transports all of us to divine heights, whether it's rock and roll or R&B or Reggae, it really is all soul music. Music, like sport, transcends all barriers of class, colour and religious conviction. It brings us together and into union with ourselves. Getting kids in touch with a deeper, inner listening is a way of opening them, and taking them as close as they may ever get on Earth to a direct experience of universal love. It's this experience of love which can lead to personal transformation and positive change on a planetary scale. Because, in the words of songwriter Andrew Lloyd Webber, "Love changes everything."

Exercise: The Magic Music Factory

Close your eyes and imagine you are standing at the gates of a big factory. You can't see in but from the outside you can hear lots of strange noises and odd musical notes. A big brass French horn above the gates starts to play and they swing open in time. You walk around the factory. It's filled with huge machines, whirring and twanging, making noises you have never heard before. A tall conductor arrives, his coat singing as he moves. He explains that this is where all the sounds and music in the world are made. He tells you that you can choose one to take home if you would like. It will be your special sound and whenever you hear it, you'll feel like you're home. What do you choose? The conductor hands you your sound in a crystal box and tells you to take very good care of it. You can open the box and listen to it anytime you like.

Languages, Accents and Dialects

Some kids manifest their audio intuition by showing a super-sense for all languages – modern and ancient. These children can grow up and use their skills in many ways across a range of different fields. Whether they are UN interpreters, anthropologists or linguists, their talents can help us understand difference and bring us closer together. If your child uses their intuition in this way try and choose a school that supports them. If you want to promote this in your child, expose them to other languages as early as possible. Research shows that listening to and speaking another language from a young age, opens up more neural pathways in the brain and increases academic outcomes across the board. So we can have multilingual, brainier and more intuitive kids!

Guided Visualisation: Audio

Close your eyes and imagine yourself in a jungle. This is no ordinary jungle – it's bewitched! As you stand below the palm trees you hear noises you have never heard before. The sound of the grass getting taller – it sounds like it's stretching. The music of flowers tinkling in the wind, each one has its own note. The big river laughs with happiness. Now open your ears a bit wider and listen to the buzz of all the tiny insects because it's not just the plants that are bewitched in this jungle – the animals are too. All the animals here can talk – its special animal magic. As you sit in the grass, you hear a swishing noise. Something is swinging through the air very fast. Suddenly a small monkey drops down beside you, from a twangy tree creeper. He says if you follow him, he will take you to someone special who wants to talk to you. You know that it's safe so you follow the monkey to a carved stone temple. There are drums coming from inside. Can you hear the bam, bam, bam? You go into the temple and inside is the beautiful rainforest queen. When she moves her hair and dress, they make the sound that raindrops make when they hit a leaf. She is the keeper of all the sounds in this jungle. She leans forward to whisper something into your ear. It might be the answer to a question you have wondered about or it might be a surprise. Whatever it is, it is magical information – just for you. And the amazing thing is she talks without speaking, but you can still understand perfectly what is being said. What does she say to you? When you have heard her, you can say thank you and say goodbye and follow the monkey back to the long grass. When you get there close your eyes. The jungle noises fade and you can hear the sounds back in the room. When you are ready, open your eyes. You can go back and talk to her anytime you like.

Chapter 5
Intuitive Feeling

Super Emotion

Intuitive feeling is the kinesthetic super-sense. This is where children use their emotions to access their intuition. Intuition and emotion are inseparable. The more we use our intuition, the more our emotional landscape will open up to us. Intuition and feeling are very similar; they both go beyond logic and the rational. If we close off our feeling, our intuition will follow. At the other end of the scale, feeling emotionally out of control can make it impossible to get clear on intuition.

The key to positively channelling this type of intuition and managing a child who accesses their intuition this way is to understand how their internal world is operating. Firstly, they are sensitive to every emotional vibration they come into contact with, which they may experience as feelings in their body. They will show a profound empathy for others, which they often feel compelled to share through feelings that are beyond words. They have an exquisite appreciation for the emotional atmosphere of any situation and a deep understanding of what everyone is truly feeling. These kids are very good at spotting the difference between what is being said and what is being felt. So if someone is saying they're fine but actually are far from it, they'll be able to feel beyond the façade. This talent to pick up emotion is possible for them, regardless of how far apart they are from the person in question.

They can literally feel over distance.

Of all the areas of intuitive intelligence, emotional intuition can be the most difficult to handle in a child. Mainly, because it can be near impossible to differentiate between how they feel and the intuition, so closely enmeshed are they. A large percentage of children who access their intuition easily, are also very emotional – it's one of the signs that a kid is intuitive. However, children who experience their intuition in this way can be extremely volatile and display 'high voltage' behaviour. This is not surprising. It takes a great deal of maturity to cope with strong emotion in a constructive way and most adults have problems with this, never mind little ones. A large part of growing up is getting a handle on feelings. So, if a child is acutely affected by emotion, both their own and others', then it's natural that they will sometimes find it difficult to separate the two and become overwrought and overwhelmed. As a result, children who *feel* intuitively will often display extreme sadness, anger, happiness and everything in between, sometimes all in the one afternoon. These are children who just seem to emote everywhere – often in a pretty dramatic way! Having a kid who moves from meltdown to merriment in two nanoseconds can feel like one giant roller coaster ride. Apart from being exhausting for them and you, it can also be difficult socially. The embarrassment factor for you and others can be high when your child is an emotional chameleon. The positive side of this is that they are normally very loving and open-hearted children who express affection easily.

"Samantha has had significant experiences through picking up people's energy. She is very sensitive to this, which has made friendships difficult because when she goes round to play, she picks up on the whole family's energy. Once she slept at a girl's house, who had a very emotionally troubled brother. She felt anxious, afraid, unsafe and unable to sleep, spending half the night crying. It turned out that the brother had stolen money from an ATM machine that same night. That was a real lesson for me, so when she says she doesn't feel comfortable with someone, I listen!! She also appears to have a lot of compassion and an ability to go straight in and feel another's pain, with wisdom and understanding far beyond her years."

- Samantha's mum, Harriet.

While this was, unfortunately, an upsetting experience for Samantha, it highlights the most important point in dealing with this super-sense. It's crucial to teach these children emotional distance. In every situation they need to be clear on two questions:

1. Is this my feeling?
and
2. What am I supposed to be getting from this?

The answers in Samantha's case would be that this is *not* her feeling – it's coming from her friend's brother and what her intuition is telling her is that she doesn't feel safe around him and should be careful. This is a core issue, because these children can often spend years not being able to distinguish their own feelings from those of other people. Not knowing the answer to these two questions can cause emotionally intuitive children to spend a lot of time feeling miserable and not knowing why. Alternatively, knowing the answers means empowered kids.

A classic example of this was a young friend of mine who suddenly felt sick while waiting in a bank queue and couldn't work out why, until he spotted the pregnant woman standing in front of him! Once he made the link he knew he wasn't actually getting ill, he was just suffering from morning sickness by proxy!

If you have an emotionally intuitive child it's essential that you demonstrate to them how to get emotional distance. Try these three strategies:

1. Set up feedback.
If they feel a powerful emotion then get them to speak it out loud. By articulating how they are feeling in that moment (e.g. 'I'm feeling angry now') they can check in with others whose emotions they might be picking up. Obviously, this is best done at home with family or with people they trust.

2. Show them how to set up a reality check for themselves.
If they've been feeling fine, then suddenly sad, then they're probably picking up on something else outside them. Just bringing the possibility of this into consciousness can help a child make the distinction.

3. Watch for overwhelm.

If you have a very young child and you think an environment or person is affecting their mood, take them to a place of neutrality.

While this form of intuition may appear 'high maintenance', it does have huge benefits for the child. Knowing what others are feeling is an amazing resource in life and work. Children who do this are naturally skilled for jobs in the caring professions or to work as therapists or with children. Being able to know that their emotions are signposts and can be used for guidance gives them a whole new way of working with feelings. And while younger children might seem like emotional hurricanes, if we can teach them how to use that emotion they will grow into empathetic and emotionally literate adults, which is a beautiful outcome.

Nurture it! Here's what you can do:

• Teach them to trust their feelings. And you should trust them too. If they feel something is wrong – act on it.

• Be vigilant about what they are exposed to, especially in the media. Disturbing news stories or drama can wreak havoc with emotionally sensitive kids.

• Spend time every day reminding your child of all the happy things in their lives – get them to focus on the positive.

• If your child is older, introduce the idea that the best way to empathetically help someone is to find ways they can help themselves.

Kids who emotionally intuit are so compassionate they energetically reach out to everyone around them – especially if they feel someone is in need. One teenager described it to me as if he just wanted to take on their load. This can lead to children becoming energetically overextended and then, they are often prone to illness. If this sounds like your child, do the following exercise once a week at bedtime to bring their energy back in. Don't worry about repeating it, kids learn by repetition – they love doing the same thing every day. They also learn by imitating so make sure you're walking your talk!!

Exercise: The Magic Force Field

Close your eyes and imagine that you have a magic force field around your body. It's bright and it's shaped like you, just like a shadow, only white and surrounding you. This is your enchanted protection. Nothing bad can come through it – only good things can get through its deflector shields. Just check it now and make sure there's nowhere it's out of shape, stretched or broken. If it has got a little baggy or moved too far out from your body then pour some more shiny magic-force juice into it and watch it spring back into place.

Picking Up Emotions in Places or Objects

Children who are emotionally intuitive can often pick up on the emotional vibration in a building or a piece of clothing or furniture. While this seems extraordinary, we do live in a vibrational universe so it makes sense that we leave behind traces wherever we have been. Usually children will feel things from the past but they can also sometimes intuit the future, getting a sense or feeling of something that is yet to happen.

When I was a young child I was often overcome by emotion, by the feelings in houses or buildings that I was visiting – especially if the buildings were historic and where I grew up they nearly all were. It was as if I absorbed it through my skin. If the feeling was sad, then I felt tragic, if it was joyful, I was ecstatic. My mother, who was uncomfortable around strong emotion, was often perplexed by me, so I soon learned to pull it in a bit. As I grew older, around nine or ten, I began to see pictures with the feelings; people arguing or a violent incident that had happened there and I began to understand why I was sensing that feeling and also that it didn't belong to me.

"Karla can pick up information about people from jewellery. It started when she was about six. She picked up a wedding ring in my dressing table, which belonged to my grandmother and told me things about her life I'd never shared with her. She slipped it on her finger and said, 'The lady who wore this made hats and lived in a big house and was lonely because her husband had got lost'. My grandmother was a milliner, she did have a large house and her husband was lost in action in World War 1."

- Karla's mum, Genevieve

Children who use this type of intuition have a very valuable gift. They have a strong emotional guidance system and can know whether or not they are going to be happy living or working somewhere; a sort of extra-sensory Feng Shui! Because they have a deep understanding of how the past can affect the present they can work as intuitive historians or detectives, gaining details and information from the past. And as they get older they can learn and teach how to clear that energy so we can live free of history. If your child is emotionally intuitive then protect them by teaching them how to shield themselves. Get them to imagine that they have a magic bubble around them that only allows in and out good feelings and emotions that make them feel safe. Explain they can use this protection any time they like.

If a child's environment is affecting them, you can teach them how do an energetic makeover. Show them how to clear old negative energy and create a positive new vibe. Turn around a gloomy space. Paint a room, burn sage, do a simple energy clearing imagining a bright white light filling all parts of the room. Throw out old furniture or fabrics and hang colourful pictures. They'll be able to feel the transformation.

Remember:

• Do keep photos and sentimental pieces of your family history around the home. Tell your child about where they are from.

• Be aware that clutter at home, but especially in junk shops or at garage sales, can be a bit full on for these kids. Think of it like energy rubbish tips. Clear out whatever you no longer need.

• Give your child the space to express their emotions – even if that feels alien to you.

• Watch for the signs that they're becoming overwrought and teach them how to self-soothe.

• Use Australian and/or Bach Flower Essences with your child. Flower essences predominantly work on emotional states, which then filter down to a physical level. They can be used on a huge range of emotional states and are particularly good for stress and anxiety. Available in drops, sprays or creams, find them in your local health food store and if you're interested in knowing how to use them for yourself, you can do a workshop.

Exercise: History Mystery

Find one or two old objects or photos and give them to your kid to play with. Then let them make up stories around them – who the people in the picture were, what they did for a living, what the object was used for. It doesn't matter if they are right – let them have fun with it.

'Gut Feelings'

Kids who intuit by emotion are usually very clear and accurate about making a call on something. This is partly because emotion is such a strong force, but also because it's less dependent on the intellect, and intuition works much better when the mind isn't too involved. When children use intuition this way, they will feel that something is right or wrong and they can be very determined about it!

"I filled out a competition form I'd found in a magazine but I kept 'forgetting' to send it. My daughter asked me every day to put it in the mail – she was sure we would win. I was scared she would be disappointed and kept avoiding posting it. Finally on the last day she begged me to send it, so I gave in.

When Naomi fixes on something, she's like a force of nature. She won't be swayed from it. Two months later I got a call telling me we'd won an all-expenses-paid trip to Europe. She's only nine and her faith in her feelings is an inspiration to me."
- Naomi's mum, Denise.

This is a very straightforward form of intuition. The challenge is not to override it with fear and doubt. Children are far better at trust than adults but we can all second-guess ourselves. Having total belief in our intuition is one of the most difficult things to cultivate and it brings up a very good question – is intuition ever wrong?

Scientists have done a great deal of research to prove that these random insights are often way off the mark. For example, if 20 people in one day get the feeling that their Grandmother has died, only a few of them might be accurate. However science doesn't measure other things, like what death or the death of that person means to the person who was thinking about it. Intuitively, it could be a nudge to put a relationship right while there's still time, for example. In my experience, intuition is infallible but we are not, and it has to come through us. Interpreting it wrongly, taking misjudged action, or letting ego get in the way can muddy the waters. Teaching children how to use their intuition in an objective way is hugely important. Separating our intuition from our desires is a skill we will continue to develop throughout our lives. Ironically we often need to be the most objective when we are least clear about something, or most fixated on a person or an issue. When ego gets tangled up with intuition then all manner of calamity can ensue. Mistakes aside, I've got into a lot more trouble ignoring my intuition than from following it.

Intuition often asks us to see a bigger picture; a broader view of outcomes. Something that initially might seem disastrous, where we acted on something and it turned out badly, can actually be a huge gift – we just need the passage of time to gain some perspective. For children who operate almost entirely in the here and now, this can be very difficult to get their heads around. Keeping a journal can help children see a pattern of success. If they do trust their judgement and it appears to go wrong, back-track with them and see if you can find a reason. Was there a bigger lesson they needed to learn?

Exercise: Sure thing!

Close your eyes and remember a time you just felt sure that you were right about something – deep down to the tip of your toes. It could have been an answer at school or when you felt for certain that something was going to turn out a particular way and then it did! Remember what it felt like to be so sure. Really feel it inside. In your imagination reach out and touch it. What does it feel like? Now just let that feeling of being sure run over you, like melted chocolate – mmm, yummy! Just let yourself feel how good it feels. Know whenever you have that scrumptious feeling you can trust yourself. When you're ready you can open your eyes.

Affinity with Nature

Children who use intuitive emotion have an enormous rapport with the natural world. These children can show gifts for horticulture – literally able to grow anything – and for caring for animals of all kinds. They will have an uncanny ability to know what a plant or pet needs and can grow up to use this sense professionally. Kids who do this can be 'weeny greenies' – strong advocates for animal rights and ecological issues from a young age.

> *"Samuel, 5, gardens intuitively. He listens to the plants and asks them where they want to go. He also talks to them as he puts them in the ground and welcomes them to the garden. If they start to die, he touches them and tries to work out what they need. He also imagines protection around them, so they won't be eaten by bugs. It's like he's feeling the landscape. My husband and I laughed about it at first but his veggies and flowers grow bigger and better than all of ours and I've found myself asking his advice down at the garden centre!"*
>
> *- Samuel's mum, Rachel.*

Connecting children with their intuition through their relationship to the environment is a win-win situation. Teaching our kids how to be eco-aware helps the planet and being outdoors is like fertilizer for intuition. Intuition and nature are interdependent. Both miraculous and around us all the time, they are the identical twins of the super-sense world. It's easy to see what they have in common. Nature has a deep knowing that is a mirror to intuition – trees intuitively know how to grow from seeds. Intuition often comes with an inbuilt sense of self-worth which is also reflected in nature – birds are not worrying about what the flowers are thinking of them. They are just doing what they do perfectly. Nature, like intuition, has great power and it has to be treated with care and great responsibility, otherwise we suffer. Nature works to keep itself in balance. It's abundant and boundless and we can work with it or against it. Nature and intuition both keep us humble – when we are in contact with them we can see that there is something bigger than ourselves. We also see how we all fit in, are all interconnected, that we all need each other and no one is more important than anyone or anything else. Nature and intuition help us understand death and re-birth, life cycles and seasons; subjects that many of us have largely lost touch with in our urban lives. If your child is using their intuition in this way, they have their finger on the pulse of life and are aligning with one of the most powerful intuitive forces there is, and one we very much need to listen to – Mother Earth.

Seven steps to naturally intuitive kids:
- Get them busy in the garden. Let them plant things and watch them grow.
- Teach them how to recycle and compost. Have a worm farm.
- Take them out into nature for walks and holidays. Become a member of your local zoo and adopt an animal.
- Show them that being 'green' starts at home. Support your local environment and get involved with greening your neighbourhood.
- Choose products that are environmentally friendly and talk to your kids about the choices you make and why.
- Give them responsibility for caring for an animal – even if it's something humble like a hermit crab.

• If your kids decide they don't want to eat meat, let them be vegetarian.

Seasons, Rhythm and Intuition

Honour the seasons. Keeping our children connected to the natural world is very important. Intuition has ebbs and flows, just like the great outdoors. Sometimes it feels strong, other times it's less insistent. Make your children aware of nature's calendar; the moon and it's phases every month and the coming and going of Winter, Summer, Spring and Autumn. Eat seasonal fruit and veggies. Do fun things that reflect the time of the year. We have lost a great deal of our awareness of these rhythms because we spend less time outside. Embrace some of Mother Nature's festivals like harvest and equinox as well as the more commercial celebrations.

Intuition Through Touch

Children who use this super sense have a heightened, extremely sensitive, sense of touch. They can often pick up dis-ease or imbalance in the body just by putting their hands on someone. If they are in an emotionally charged situation they may have strong physical sensations in their own body. Parts of them can tingle, go hot, cold or numb, or feel heavy. Again it's essential to separate what's going on for them and what they are picking up from around them. The most profound experience of this I ever had was when:

"I used to work as a nurse in theatre recovery. Once I was looking after a little boy who had his tonsils out. He seemed fine after the surgery but I kept delaying his return to the ward. We were very busy and I was under a lot of pressure to move him on. I asked the doctor to check him twice but there were no obvious problems. Still I stayed with him. Every time I checked his vital signs I felt dizzy, my head hurt and I wanted to lie down. Just as the other staff were questioning my professional judgement, and I was wondering whether I needed to go home sick, his blood pressure suddenly dropped to dangerous

levels. He was rushed back into theatre, where they found that he had been slowly bleeding into his stomach the whole time. If he'd gone back to the ward, it would almost certainly have gone unnoticed and he could have died."

"Alexi, 9, met this woman in the street and said he was sorry her hands were sore. She was astonished, she had just been diagnosed with arthritis, though her hands looked normal. Later when I quizzed him, he said he had felt pain in his fingers at the same time."
- Alexi's mum, Deborah.

If your child does what Alexi's mum describes in the example above very often, use the distancing techniques I described earlier in this chapter. If they are picking up powerful feelings in their body, get them to talk to that part of themselves and find out what information their body is trying to share with them. Also teach them to shield themselves so they are not swept away by a tsunami of feeling from other people's physical ailments.

If they are open to it, introduce them to basic massage and Reiki – a Japanese form of energetic hands-on healing – as a way of channelling their intuition. Then if they pick up dis-ease in someone they can use their Reiki for direct or distance healing. Children who use this super-sense usually respond very well to alternative health practices when they are ill, because they innately understand the rationale behind them. If this describes your child, consider embracing holistic as well as conventional approaches to wellbeing for them. Children who intuit this way will often gravitate towards the healing arts anyway, both personally and professionally.

Guided Visualisation: Super Feeling

Close your eyes and imagine that you are standing beside a beautiful deep river. The clear water sparkles in the sunlight. You put your hand in and it feels cool. You feel very happy and safe here. There are ripples on the surface of the water and a silvery fish pops its head out. It has a gold ring in its mouth and it drops it into your hand. As you feel it next to your skin you know that this is a magic ring and if you wear it, you can swim underwater just like a fish. You slip it on your finger and jump into the river. You were right! You can swim and breathe just like a fish!. You can feel the smooth water running past your body, the swish of the riverweed as it tickles your legs and the hard, round river pebbles in the sand at the bottom. As you explore around the rocks you watch tiny minnows darting like quicksilver in the deeper pools. As they move, you feel the water move in waves against you. You understand that they are scared of you and that makes you feel sad, so you smile at them so they know you don't want to hurt them. One little fish, braver than the rest, flicks its tail and comes over to you. His shiny scales keep changing colour like a kaleidoscope. You feel that he's nervous and he becomes yellow. Then you smile at him and he relaxes and his colour changes to green. You realise his colours change with his feelings. You ask him if he wants to explore with you and he turns bright blue! Something up ahead catches your eye, something glinting in the water. You swim up to it with a flick of your feet, your friend, the minnow, just behind you. There, stuck in the fine sand, is a chest made of shell. It's shiny and translucent. You dive down to get to it. As you touch the box, you feel a tingling in your hand that stretches up your arm and through your whole body. You have a feeling of excitement. You know there is something really good in there. You also know, just from touching it, that's it very old and that it fell over the side of a boat that sailed down the river a very long time ago. At the front of the box is a small catch and you open it. The little fish beside you is turning all sorts of colours at once, with excitement and nervousness. You open the scalloped lid and at the bottom is a huge, shiny pearl. When you pick it up you feel very calm and you know everything is always going to be all right. Feeling very peaceful you put it back and say goodbye to Mr Minnow. Then you swim back to the surface. The world looks and feels like it's bursting with happiness. You climb out and slip the magic ring in your pocket. You can swim back to the pearl and hold it anytime you like.

Chapter 6
Intuitive Knowing

Super Thought

Intuitive knowing is, perhaps, one of the easiest forms of intuition to understand and recognise, because virtually all of us will have experienced it for ourselves in some way. Those moments when we have an idea that comes out of nowhere, that we know is valuable, is an example of intuitive knowing. It's also a very accessible form of intuition and I think we accept it so readily as it initially appears to have come out of our own thoughts. Interestingly when we examine this, we usually find it comes from a space between our thinking – that it actually drops in between our thoughts and that it is, on closer inspection, coming from beyond reason.

If your child is experiencing this form of intuition, then they will be getting frequent flashes of insight or 'aha' moments – thoughts that contain guidance and wisdom. These can be incredibly subtle and about very ordinary things. A knowing it would be better to pass on fizzy drink and have some water, or to phone a friend immediately. In fact the ordinariness of this intuition can cause us to overlook it, because we might be expecting something more dramatic. Intuitive counsellor and author, Sonia Choquette, sums this up perfectly in her book, *Vitamins for the Soul*, when she says, "It doesn't have to be a big deal to follow your intuition. In fact intuition rarely is a big deal – it's more often a series of unending little deals that make life easier and more magical." For me, this kind of intuition is an everyday occurrence:

"This is the bread and butter of my intuition – I use it every day. 'Speak up about this', 'drive this way', 'eat this for dinner' – it's like a talk-back radio show! Sometimes it can be about such apparently trivial things, like whether I buy fruit from one store, rather than another. I've actually learned not to question it any more, I take it so much for granted now that I can't imagine life without it – it's like I'm fitted with an internal GPS navigation device that's always telling me where to go!"

If you want to introduce intuition to children (and grown ups) this is a great way to begin because it's so easy to use. Start by teaching your kids to pay attention to the small stuff – little insights. As they say, God is in the detail. Point out that these tiny bursts of guidance can add up to a lot. And as Louis' story below shows, these little nudges from the universe can actually be a big deal.

"My son Louis, 4, was in the back of the car and we were driving through our local suburb. I was late and had the foot down. He said, almost in passing, 'Mum, don't go so fast there might be boys and girls on the street'. I immediately slowed down and seconds later a football hit my windscreen and a kid ran out after it. What struck me most was how matter of fact he had said it – I could have easily dismissed it."
- Louis' mum, Fiona.

Another example of this style of intuition is when kids get strong 'hunches' around situations and choices. Often they will articulate these hunches spontaneously, as they come up: 'I don't want to go to that party' or 'I'd rather go to cricket camp this summer'. When they do this it will be marked by two qualities: How crystal-clear they seem about it, even if they have barely given the topic a moment's thought before now, and how it goes against what we might have imagined their choice would have been. These hunches tend to show a maturity that go beyond what we think our kids are capable of, and can surprise parents. Indeed the term, 'out of the blue', might have been coined for this type of intuition. Here's one example of this type of hunch that happened to me:

"I had a lot of freedom when I was young and was pretty adventurous. One

day I was asked out to play by a group of local kids. At some point they wanted to head off to the river- side. I knew I wasn't allowed, but normally that wouldn't have stopped me! However on that day I said, 'No'. I just knew it wasn't the right choice. I think it would be fair to say, that making that decision was very out of character for me. That evening, I heard that the little three-year-old sister of an older boy had fallen into the river and drowned when they were larking about. Even though I wasn't older than six at the time, I understood very clearly that if I had not heeded that feeling, the day could have ended very differently for me; that it could have been me that pushed the envelope too far that day."

"Tania, 6, had been desperate to go to the fun-fair all weekend but had been sick. She was devastated at missing out and had whined continuously about it, driving us all mad! On the Sunday, she was a bit better and we wanted to give her the chance to go, so her dad asked her what she felt was best. Without hesitation she said she needed to sleep and went back to bed. I don't know who was more shocked, though I knew she had made a wise choice. I'm not sure how to explain this exactly but as she said it, the decision seemed to come from some other part of her."
- Tania's aunt, Nicoletta.

Simple though it may be, this type of intuition is significant because it's the same intuition that will, in a few years time, advise your kids not to take drugs, get into cars with drivers who've been drinking, or have unprotected sex. Teaching them to listen to it now can save a lot of heartache down the line for them and you. And the beauty of it is that it comes from within them – so it's harder for them to throw it out as the rantings of some overprotective parent (that's you by the way!) If you introduce them now to the idea that this knowing is something they can respect and trust, then when they're out in the world making decisions that really count they are more likely to rely on what's worked for them before.

This type of intuition is also often responsible for sending little hints and direction around your kid's life purpose. Those little ideas that they get to join a club, take up a hobby or choose a certain subject at school are all part of a mosaic of carefully planted, intuitive suggestions and opportunities that will eventually lead them to their bliss in work and life. There are no accidents with intuition. If you look back over the course of your life and see the amount of serendipity that has brought you to where you are today, you'll be astounded. If you are reading this and thinking, 'Well that sounds great, but my kid has no idea what they want to do,' or even, 'How can I help them recognise their purpose when I've never even figured out my own?', then relax. Everything your child needs to know lies within them (the same goes for you too, by the way!). Secondly, timing is everything. Intuition is never late or early – it arrives exactly when it needs to. Some kids are just born with a mission. They've always known where they're headed and they just go after it. They don't need help to work it out because they are on track and focussed. For them, this intuition is useful in making the best choices as they travel with a determined eye on the horizon. Other kids need longer; they need to experiment and explore before they get an idea of where they want to go. While they do this, their intuition will keep popping up to stop them from getting lost. Either way, it doesn't matter how it unfolds – it's perfect for your child. The important thing is that wherever they are at, they keep checking in with their intuition.

If the question of what your child wants to do in the future arises, then work through these five purpose points:
- What would you do if you could do anything?
- How does that feel when you say that?
- Is there anything that's stopping you?
- What needs to happen for there to be nothing in your way?
- Close your eyes and picture yourself doing what you love.

While intuition is always relevant, there can be times when our children may get a knowing about subjects or situations, beyond what they have been told or understand and which we might prefer they didn't know about...

"When I was a young teenager, I told my dad that two people in our church were having a relationship. I had no proof of this, and both of them were married to other people, so it was an explosive revelation. The man was my father's best friend and naturally he was upset by what I had told him. My dad quizzed me hard, but all I could say was that it had just come to me and

I knew it was true. My father was angry and asked me not to repeat it. Some months later their affair was revealed and the community was split apart." (Author)

This story from my adolescence raises a question that any child who uses their intuition – and their parents – will have to face at some point. And that is, why am I getting specific information when it doesn't seem directly relevant to me? In my story I

> **"Timing is everything. Intuition is never late or early – it arrives exactly when it needs to."**

can see in retrospect – though it wasn't clear at the time – that it was about me learning to stick up for my intuition. It was also an opportunity for my father to stop denying what I could do and how his friend was behaving. In this way my intuition was being used to help both me and my dad grow and learn. Often when intuition flows, it's for the benefit of more than the person it comes through. There are many other reasons why intuition may come through, apparently uninvited or unasked for. The most common ones are:

• There is danger for someone your child is close to that can be averted.

• There is something in the other person's situation that your child can learn from.

• They are picking up on everyone around them and need to filter selectively. For help with this try the exercise below.

When information comes to our children about other people, it can provide a good opportunity to discuss some of the ethical issues around intuition. How and why our kids use their intuition will influence not only how much they can connect with it, but also how much it serves them and others. My personal approach is that I use my super-senses to harm none (including myself), and to love all. Ultimately though, the relationship and the values our kids apply to their intuition is a personal decision; all we can do is bring awareness to it and point them in the right direction.

Exercise: Magic Mail

Close your eyes and imagine that you are inside your head. It's an amazing place filled with books and fantastic games and boxes of ideas. Wow, you can have a lot of fun in here! Keep walking to the very front of your forehead. Right in the centre, high up, you will see a glass chute. Every few minutes a gold envelope with a scarlet stamp drops down like they're being posted. There are so many golden letters with your name on them, each with a special message – just for you! But wait, something's gone wrong, suddenly there are hundreds of letters flying down the chute – going everywhere and they've all got other people's names on them. You run around to pick up the letters but it's gone crazy. Then you notice a lever by the side of the chute and pull it. Whew! The mail has stopped but you are knee deep in gold envelopes! 'I wish they'd all go back to where they belong', you think to yourself...and immediately they disappear – now that's a neat trick! So you decide to try it again. Walk around your brain and see what you can make happen just by thinking it. It's very cool. What can you do? Now it's time to come home, but you have to make sure that the mail doesn't go crazy again. So you go to the chute and think, 'I only want to get letters if they're for me and when I really need to know something'. As soon as you think it a blue spark flashes in the air and one giant letter slides down the chute. You open it and it says, 'You got it!' Knowing that you've taken care of that now, you can open your eyes. Remember, you can try making things happen just by thinking about them anytime you like.

Divine Inspiration

Children who use this type of intuition will often be inspired and inspire others with their amazing ideas that again, seem to come out of the blue. Frequently it presents as highly individual thinking – the world of their thoughts is usually extraordinarily creative and imaginative. This can be seen in creative play when children have ingenious ideas for games or experimentation. Interestingly, when a group of children get together to play, a group synthesis can happen, where intuition and inspiration starts to bounce from one to another and they build on it together. This is incredibly exciting to watch, or to be part of. In fact, it actually energises children – intuition is thrilling! This type of intuition has a group consciousness. People all over the world having the same great idea at the same time, or projects having global synchronicity are good examples of this. When kids play together in groups, we are seeing this in microcosm.

It's not just in generating ideas that these super-sense kids excel, they can also integrate new ideas and technology at a rate far faster than their parents could or can. You only have to see a three-year-old playing with a mobile phone or *iPod* to see this in reality – Generation Intuitives are far more sophisticated than we were.

If you want to encourage intuitive inspiration in your children – leave them alone! No, really! Obviously all children need adult input and time to play with family, but intuition, inspired play and ideas happen best when children are not organised by adults but left to structure something for themselves. There is a school of educational thought that believes as soon as you entertain children, you remove the opportunity for learning. The same can also be said for inspiration. Intuition thrives in open, formula-free scenarios. Ditto for toys. There are many fabulous, educational, interactive, stimulating toys on the market but intuition flourishes equally as well, if not better with simple play situations. A sand-pit and some blocks or a cardboard cubby house are just as effective. This is one of the most effortless ways of building intuition because kids get to experience it doing the thing they enjoy most – playing. And children who get to experiment in this way are also filling a huge warehouse of confidence. The knowing that they can be the source of creativity with ideas that just pop into their heads – that they don't have to look to anyone else for it – how priceless is that?!

Once you've got them started, this form of intuition can be very addictive. Just keep in mind these few DOs and DON'Ts:

• When they do have an idea don't crush it with an adult opinion (we've all done it – oops). What might look very ordinary to us, might be very precious to a child, and who knows what they are building on. I've been having experiences since I was three that have led to me writing this book.

• Do give them the freedom to make mistakes and a mess. A child learns in the opposite way from an adult. We normally start a project in our heads, then after planning it, begin. Children start by doing and out of that activity, ideas occur. This is how intuition through play happens. Don't worry if it all seems a bit chaotic, all intuitive geniuses have to start somewhere!

• Do teach them to focus and follow through. Some children can have so many ideas they don't know where to start or how to finish.

Too Much Too Soon?

A really common dilemma for parents is to know how much information they should give to their child about intuition. Younger children especially can seem a little haphazard in relation to their intuition and it might be hard to work out if they are really experiencing something or making it up some of the time. They might see auras one day but not the next for example. In general it's best to let the child lead their learning. Be reassured that in an open environment they will ask the questions they need to, when the time is right for them.

Exercise: The Magic Play-dom

Turn off the TV and banish computer games for a whole week (you might want to try this for yourselves too) and have play-overs at home or at the park instead. Then have a whole weekend where nothing is organised for the kids. No sports, no parties, no trips to the movies. Once the initial disorientation and irritation passes see how they move to create spontaneously. Praise them for every idea they have.

Communicating By Thought

For some children this group intuition goes further and they can actually send their thoughts to others and communicate that way. Again, many children will do this without even thinking about it. It can happen randomly but usually it's between siblings, close friends and family. The closer the relationship the easier it seems to be. It's not surprising then, that twins sharing thoughts and being able to pick up on each other's thinking is well documented.

> *"My son Carl used to say to me, 'Mum, how come I know what people are going to say?' It can be very frustrating, as a mother, when he knows what I'm thinking! It's like we're both connected into the same power source."*
> *- Carl's mum, Kim*

This form of intuition is relatively common but in general it is usually used in a basic, quite haphazard way. I believe that's because, unless two people are on the same wavelength it takes a great deal of focus and intention. But the point is it can be done and it can be useful. Children can pick up if someone is being less than honest with them or they can come by information that might be useful to them. Let your child know it's possible and suggest they have some fun giving it a go. If they experience this more often, then make sure that they are only receiving and sending thoughts that are positive and useful. If you feel that's not the case then get them to imagine that they have a big tap inside their head, which controls the flow of information, and they can turn it on or off when they choose.

Crystal-Clear Thoughts

While intuition comes from a realm beyond thought, what we think can influence our intuition. Our thoughts are incredibly powerful and we create our reality by what we think. It's important then to focus our thoughts on the positive because negative thinking can reduce intuitive flow. The impact of negative thinking was recently proved in a series of astonishing experiments by Japanese scientific researcher and healer, Dr. Masaru Emoto. Emoto, in his ground-breaking work, discovered that water which was exposed to negative words or thoughts, formed incomplete and deformed crystals when frozen. Water that had loving words spoken to it showed brilliant, complex and colourful snowflake patterns. Emoto has also shown, through his stunning photography that music, words written on paper, pictures and photographs all have an impact on the crystal structure of water. Emoto argues that since people are 70 percent water and the Earth is also 70 percent water, we can heal the planet and ourselves by consciously expressing love, goodwill and gratitude. H_2O anyone?

Guided Visualisation: Intuitive Knowing
Mountain of Secrets

Close your eyes and imagine you are standing at the bottom of a very high mountain. It's so high the top disappears into the clouds. You know that at the top is a sacred palace and you've been told that's where all the secrets of the world are kept. You want to go and find them out. You start to climb the mountain. The track is very difficult but you keep going. As you get near the top, you feel like you can almost touch the sun. Then you get to the edge of the mountain. The path stops and there's no way to go higher. You look up and think, 'If only I could fly!' Suddenly you are soaring into the sky. You can see for miles and you see you have two powerful wings stretching on either side. You are an eagle! It's amazing to be so high soaring on the warm air. You can easily swoop down into the palace. You land in the courtyard and shape-shift back to your body. The place seems to be deserted but you get the idea that there is someone here. Just as you think this, a gigantic, scaly dragon appears. It's his job to guard the secrets. You think it might be a good idea to turn into an eagle again and fly away! But the dragon says he's bored, no one ever comes to visit and he would love to play with you. He promises not to singe your bottom if you win! You agree and spend all afternoon playing the best games together. Dragons know a lot of cool games and you think up exciting ones too. Can you see what you are playing? Then before you know it, it's getting dark and you have to get home for dinner. You say goodbye, but oh no! You forgot to find out any secrets! The dragon roars a fiery laugh and tells you that knowing how to be friends and making up new ways to have fun together is one of the biggest secrets there is! He does share with you one other secret though. That's the invisible cable car that brings you back down to the bottom of the mountain in an instant. You can come back and make believe with the dragon any time you like just by thinking about it.

Chapter 7
Physical Intuition

This is the body super-sense, which is accessed by tapping into a body knowing or intelligence. This chapter explores the different aspects of this physical intuition and how it can manifest in our children.

The Body as a Barometer

Children who experience their intuition on a physical level use the body as a barometer through which they sense their inner and outer world. They are literally having a dialogue with their body, whether they are conscious of it or not. For them, their centre of wisdom is in the physical, and it speaks to them through the physical body. This can manifest in a number of ways but it will always come back to the body. Most commonly children will have a physical sensation somewhere in their body, which again, with or without awareness, they will be able to interpret as having meaning. An example of this is when the child senses danger and feels a contraction in their gut or in their chest. Children who use their intuition in this way are like mini sensors with a constant bio-feedback mechanism. Their body is telling them all the time whether someone can be trusted or how close they should go to the edge of a cliff. Not to be confused with instinct, physical intuition gives specific information and advice. Children who favour this form of intuition are easy to pick out. They generally are very physically orientated and can instantly point to where they are feeling things in their body if you ask them. Often this sensation will be accompanied by an emotion. For these children, intuition, emotion and physical sensation are all interrelated.

"I was visiting a house and sitting in the lounge I had this pain and tightness in my chest and felt incredibly sad at the same time. Later I found out the woman, who was in her early fifties and owned the house, had had a heart attack in that room after her husband had left her. I put my hand on my heart and it told me that she had to sell the house and move on if she wanted to heal. Soon after I got the chance to share this with her, but she said she just couldn't let go of the property or the past. She died of a cardiac arrest a few months later." (Author)

This dramatic story is a textbook example of physical intuition. I got a feeling in my body, related to an emotion that was being triggered by a past event, which contained valuable information about the future for the person it involved. It also shows that you can pass on intuitive wisdom but it's up to the free will and choice of the person receiving it to decide what they do with it. This is a very important lesson to get across to Gen I kids. Often when they feel they know something about someone, they feel very responsible for the outcome. So it's good to point out, as someone once did to me, that we're not God. All we can do is be the best messenger we can. After that, it's out of our hands.

While I had this particular experience as an adult, I had many similar episodes as a child. This is an excellent form of intuition because we all have a body and we can all use it for guidance. Children who get their intuition this way can, ironically, not take very good care of their bodies. They can tend to overlook some of their physical limits because their super-sense can make them feel invincible and they are generally pretty physical kids. This particularly, but not exclusively, applies to boys. So, educate them on good health choices around their body and show them how to pace themselves.

A major block to physical intuition is shame around any part of the body. If a child is cut off from part of their body because of guilt or shame they can't use it to feel. Teaching our kids to really love their bodies no matter what type of body they've got is very important.

If they are feeling strong physical sensations, then show them how to know if what they feel in their body belongs to them or someone else. They can do this by just asking that part of their body to say 'yes' or 'no' to them. You can also teach them to recognise their own body's feedback. So for example if the hairs on the back of their neck stand up when they get excited, they can use that as a signpost that they are headed in the right direction when they are making a decision. Alternatively, a sick feeling in the stomach probably means it's not such a great idea.

Intuition and Diet

There's been a great deal of useful information written about intuitive kids, their deep sensitivity to what they eat and how it affects their behaviour. However there is another relationship between food and intuition that we need to understand. Sugar, artificial chemicals and additives, highly processed and fast foods are not only bad for our children's physical wellbeing and conduct, they do nothing for their intuitive self either. It's a fact that if their systems are loaded with junk for fuel, they will be less efficient conductors of intuition. Regardless of how good your child's diet is, it's basically impossible to keep the food they eat as pure as we would probably like it to be. Virtually all the food we can buy has been added to, or treated in some way. Given that our children, from the point they start to eat solids, probably never have a day where their system is not influenced by some artificial ingredient, then the reality is, that their intuition is constantly being compromised by their diet. It's not my intention to add any more parent guilt on this topic. We all have to live in the real world and I believe we are all doing the best we can. I don't know a mother who doesn't try daily to get her kids to eat more veggies. However if you are serious about encouraging your child's intuitive skills you may have to look at what they are putting in their mouths. Drinking lots of water and eating even a slightly better diet can make intuition jump up a big notch.

Kinesiology for Kids

One of the most direct ways that you can show your kid how to use their body for guidance is the use of muscle testing. The use of muscle testing to get feedback on what is happening in the body was developed forty years ago by American Chiropractor Dr. George Goodheart. The underlying belief is that the body is like a bio-computer which reacts to everything it experiences and can actually tell us exactly what supports or aggravates it. There is extensive scientific documentation of amazing blind tests which show how muscles go weak in the presence of artificial sweeteners but stay strong when exposed to natural sugars. In efficient and unbiased hands, muscle testing is a way to always get to the truth of what's going on in the body. The body doesn't lie and everything we think or feel is reflected in it. If you want to give it a try, do the next exercise.

Exercise: Magic Muscles

To have fun muscle testing with your child get them to stand with their arm stretched out to the side of their body at shoulder level. Place two fingers on their wrist and get them to say something you both know is false. "I am Mickey Mouse" is a good example. Next get the,m to say something that's true, for example, "I am seven years old." When they say the false statement you should easily be able to press their hand down. When it's true they should be able to resist you. You can then use their body to get feedback on any question. Just remember to get them to ask the question simply and for themselves. A statement like, "It's good for me to stay home from school today" works better than a question like, 'Should I go to school?'. It's like magic. This exercise can cause a lot of giggling and it's still very authentic. If your kid has a specific emotional or physical problem and you want to try it at the hands of a professional, make an appointment with your local kinesiologist who is trained specifically to do this.

Sporting Genius

Apart from this impressive connection with the physical body, intuition expressed this way often also translates in a physical genius for sport, performance or dance. Top athletes or experts in a whole range of physical disciplines often experience an internal, bodily knowing about where the ball will land ahead of time, or which way they need to move in order to outsmart their opponent or perform at their very best.

> *"My friend's son Tyler showed his physical fearlessness and flair from the moment he could run, which was approximately two seconds after he could walk. He could climb higher and kick harder than any of his contemporaries. Now aged eight, he's naturally brilliant at all sports and it's clear from watching him that he is physically intuitive – he just knows in a deep body wisdom way that he can do it. It's not just talent it's a phenomenon which makes the hair on the back of your neck stand up when you observe it in action. Tyler not only thinks with his body, when he's moving, he is his body. It's truly a thing of beauty to watch."* (Author)

Boys especially feel comfortable expressing their intuition this way, mirroring as it does male values around the body and sport. However, girls who want to play soccer and boys who want to ballet dance are also part of this equation! There's no doubt that we can't all be like David Beckham or Cathy Freeman but there are ways of nurturing this super-sense for kids on all parts of the physical intuitive curve. If you want to encourage it in your child, expose your kid to lots of different types of physical activities and make sure the fun quota is high. If your child shows particular interest in a physical activity, invest in training if possible. Take a deep breath and encourage them in whatever it is they develop a passion for – even if they want to learn to walk the high wire. You sometimes need nerves of steel to parent a physically intuitive child!

Apart from the chance of raising an Olympic medal winner, there are some clear-cut advantages of supporting this type of intuition beyond having a fitter, healthier body and a life-long love of sport. There's a sense of oneness with others. Like music, sport and physical performance transcend barriers of race, culture and creed. They also honour qualities of discipline and human achievement. If our bodies are temples, using them intuitively to excel in this way honours the magnificence of who we are and gives permission for others to do the same. Great athletes have the power to make the whole world stand and cheer with exuberant joy. There is something divine in watching the best of the best. It lights a flame in all our hearts and inspires us to be the most we can be. Physically intuitive kids can inspire others on a scale that most advertising execs can only dream of! One caution though, it's important that they learn that healthy competition is good but a burning desire to win at any cost normally closes down, or seriously compromises physical intuition. Overtraining and cheating are the two classic side effects. Beware of pushing your super-sense child. Rather teach your child to use their physical intuition to guide them about how to develop their sportsmanship with integrity and in a healthy, balanced way.

Exercise: Field of Dreams

Close your eyes and imagine yourself dressed in the outfit/kit of your favourite sport/dance. You are waiting for your turn at the world championships. You are in a huge auditorium/stadium/stage. The stands are packed with thousands of spectators and many more people around the world are watching on TV. It's your turn next and you are pretty nervous but you've trained for a long time to be here and you want to give it your best shot. Now it's your turn to step into the centre. Your legs are a bit wobbly and your heart is beating in your chest. The audience goes quiet. Then you start to play/race/dance and everything else goes out of your mind. You can feel your body move just as it should, without you even having to think about it. It feels like a kind of magic. Everything around you is a blur, the noise, the lights, the people – it all fades away. All you can feel is your body moving better than it ever has. There's nothing you can't do. You can jump higher, run faster, flip, spin and throw better than you ever have before. Then before you know it, your time is up and everyone is standing cheering and shouting. You know it was the best you could have done. Your body is tingling and your heart is beating and you feel so happy. You are the world champion – hurrah! Now open your eyes and know you can come back to this feeling anytime you like.

Connection to Physical Reality

Kids who use intuition in this way always know what's happening in their immediate world usually before it happens. They exhibit a physical hyper-vigilance – where some part of them is always alert to change in their environment.

"When Simon walks through the front door of my office he knows if someone has been there and who it was – he can sense the physical change in the atmosphere. It's totally amazing. It's like the space has been disturbed and he gets this communication instantly through his skin."
- Simon's dad, Jeremy

Children who use this super-sense are getting information three-dimensionally, all at the same time in any given situation. Data about their environment, how they feel and the sensations in their body are pouring in continuously. So a kid might feel that there is danger in the situation they find themselves in, and at the same time feel a constriction in their chest, feel scared, and know that they need to stand very still and make no noise. All of this happens instantaneously and children who use physical intuition will, from a very early age, be able to discern the difference between these messages instantly.

"It sometimes feels like I have a invisible perimeter fence around me and I get signals before anyone gets close. I can tell before people draw up outside my house, phone or knock on the door, and I often sense who they are. This even extends to the weather; I know in my body when storms are coming and have even got a powerful sense when a large tragedy, like a terrorist bombing or natural disaster is about to happen, even if it's on the other side of the world. It's an intuitive radar." *(Author)*

This combination of physical knowing and the powerful connection with the physical world can help these super-sense kids survive in extreme situations. The have an ability to constantly transcend physical limitations and pain in an extraordinary way. For this reason when they get older they can be physical risk takers. Teens who gravitate towards extreme sports and hobbies like base jumping are usually physical intuitives. Stretching the boundaries of the body is part of who they are, just don't let them run their bodies too far.

If your kid uses their intuition in this way, encourage them to relax. Being constantly aware is exhausting – make sure they have some down time. Bring your children's awareness to how their surrounds are affecting them. If a location is overwhelming them, get out of there. While children do use this for picking up good vibes, this type of intuition normally serves as an early warning system. Its effectiveness is guaranteed because their bodies will move immediately into response. It can be a powerful force for protection so it's wise to take it seriously.

Exercise: The Magic Scanner

Close your eyes and imagine you have a magic scanner. If you wave it over your body it will tell you how you are feeling. Give it a go. What does it say? Tired, happy, hungry? Now ask the scanner to point to a part of your body where you feel relaxed and safe. It might be your belly or it might be your bottom – it doesn't matter as long as you can feel it. Now pretend you can go to that part of your body and feel that feeling of being safe. It might feel like being home, cuddling your favourite toy or being with Mum or Dad. Let yourself really feel how good it feels to be secure and know that everything is going to be all right. Feel your breaths going in and going out and as you do, let that feeling of being safe wash all over your body. When you can feel it all over, you can open your eyes. And remember, if you feel scared you can come back to this feeling anytime you like.

Gifted Performers

Children who are drawn to dance, acting and other performing arts are creating intuitively with their bodies. They can also intuit new forms of physical expression. Kids who have talents with comedy, mime, drama, movement and circus skills are usually drawing on this physical super-sense. They often have the power to deeply move audiences and will be described as having physical presence or being a natural performer. If you want to nurture this in your child you can:

• Encourage their inner entertainer. Take them to drama classes – performance is also fabulous for boosting self-confidence.
• Let them play a lot of make believe games as different characters – a good dress up box is fantastic for this.
• Make puppets and masks and create little shows with toys.
• Take them to see performance of all types.
• Dance, Dance, Dance! Dancing, like music and drumming, opens up the body and soul. Whirling, trance dance, chakra dance, Nia dance are just some of the types of dance used for healing. They encourage us to commune with our bodies and the sacred in and out of us. Kids who dance get to feel this connection. Get them into it!

"Naomi showed her gift for performance from the age of three. By the age of five she was busking, dancing and singing with her sister (and her parents' supervision) in our local main street and making a lot of money! She's a total natural. She can't help but entertain. When she's performing, she's in her element – it's as if she plugs into some super-circuit of energy. When she's on, she shines with happiness. What's most amazing is that Naomi has a physical disability but when she's performing she totally transcends it, to the point where you don't even see it anymore. It's pure alchemy."
- Talia, Naomi's aunt

Being able to make people, laugh, cry, gasp, sing along and tap their feet through performance is a great gift for the child and for all of us who get to be near it. Intuitive artistry is perhaps the most joyful of all the super-senses because it brings humanity together through pure entertainment and delight.

Guided Visualisation: Physical Intuitives

Close your eyes and imagine that you are in a space rocket. You are hurtling through the blackness, past satellites and meteors. Feel the rocket shake your body as you take off, deep into the universe. Now you push a button and accelerate to light speed...whooooah! You are pushed back into the seat and every part of you is vibrating. You can feel your heart beating with excitement. Remember to take big deep breaths. Outside you pass galaxies and then suddenly, on the horizon, you see the planet you're headed for. The rocket lands with a bit of bump. The doors open and out you step, safe in your space suit. The atmosphere is affecting your body. It can do amazing things. It can float and fly and jump huge distances or up high into the outer atmosphere. You jump so high a shooting star zooms past you – watch out! But it's okay because you knew it was coming before you saw it and you ducked to get out of the way. Smart, huh? Then you realise you can stretch and twist your body like rubber. You can grow tall, shrink to be teeny tiny, be fat or thin. It's really funny. You just have to think it and it happens - your body knows what to do. And the brilliant part is you never feel tired. Feel yourself leap and somersault and dance in space. Then you see a bag sitting on the ground. It's got, 'Magic Space Dust' written on it. You wonder if it's safe but you get the sense that it is. It's like a warm feeling in your tummy. You sprinkle some on your head and then things get very interesting! Your body can turn invisible or into water – that feels funny – or light as the air. Wow! You are floating and can even turn into fire – you're an inferno! There's nothing you can't be. You spend the morning being all the things you can think of. Then you start up the rocket and come home. You leave the space dust up there. Well, except for the little bit that you put in your pocket. You never know when you might need it! You can use it any time you like.

Chapter 8
Intuitive Healing

This is the healing super-sense. Children who are in touch with this super-sense are often very aware of their bodies and exactly what they need to be healthy. Some children also have an intuitive ability to heal themselves and others. This chapter looks into the different ways that this super-sense can show up in our children and how we can encourage its development.

Inner Holistic Knowing

Children can show healing intuition from a very young age. This can be, quite simply, the innate understanding of what they need to maintain their wellbeing. They might be drawn to certain foods or refuse food for a time. They may ask to go to bed – a miracle for most parents! Or they might choose to miss out on something or forego lollies. In these cases they are intuitively listening to their bodies. This inner knowing of what their body needs to heal can be present from the time they are babies.

> *"When Alex was less than two years old, his speech stopped. We thought it was regression with Lila, his sister, being born. On Mother's Day, we were at a shopping centre and he picked up a crystal from a stall. He stood there and put it to his throat. I bought it for him. When I looked it up, it turned out to be turquoise, which is for speech. I was blown away. After that I took him to see an energy healer and his speech improved. I know now not to ignore*

him but to put my trust in his knowing. It's not that I'm excluding medical information, that would be negligent, but we've been seeing a lot of results with alternative health."
- Alex's mum, Amanda

I believe all children are born with the ability to know what's best for them from a health point of view, but children with this super-sense will have a much stronger sense of it. If you want to encourage this in your child, the first thing you must do is prevent their intuition from being undermined. Pretty much as soon as your baby is born, both of you are faced with a line of health professionals with advice about what they require. Obviously if your child is ill and requires medical attention, you should see your health practitioner. Conventional medicine certainly has its place. As an alternative health practitioner friend pointed out, if your arm is hanging off, you can't Reiki it back on! We need hospitals and GPs and nurses. However we also need to teach our children to listen to their bodies and give them confidence that they know their bodies better than anyone else and that they can create health and avoid dis-ease for themselves. A naturopath that I knew once made the comment that if we take our child to see the doctor every time they are sick, they quickly learn that they are powerless to heal. Empowering our kids to know when their system is out of balance and to take action before it gets to be a bigger problem is the key. This might sound unremarkable but it's an inner skill that most adults have forgotten how to use. So many times we get sick or take longer to heal because we ignore our own body's wisdom. It's *so* important to give your child the space to do this, even if it doesn't immediately fit in with your routine for the day. Every time you do, you let your child know that you trust them and in turn they learn to trust themselves.

Building the trust – Here's what you can do:
• Research and use alternative health for childhood ailments when appropriate. Homeopathy and naturopathy are good places to start but there are dozens to choose from. Find a holistic modality which you feel works for your child. Apart from being non-invasive they will involve your child in their healing path.

• Teach your child and yourself about Reiki – do a basic course.

• Follow the rhythms of your child's body – even if it doesn't fit in to the daily schedule. Extend this to what they eat and drink. As much as is realistic, let your child eat when they are hungry. Many eating disorders have their genesis in getting out of touch with the body's needs.

• Involve your child in their own healing journey. Let them give you feedback about what's going on for them. Take away passivity and be an advocate for them. Stand up for your own opinion with health practitioners. Health is still an area where we doubt ourselves and need to take back our power. The best way to teach a child to honour their own intuition is to follow your own. No one knows your child better than you. When our own children are sick, it can be a very fast route to fear and second-guessing ourselves, even if, like me you are a trained health professional. When my son Callan was two, he got gastro. I had my in-laws of the time staying with me and they kept telling me he was fine. My intuition told me things were bad but I ignored it because I didn't want to be seen to be causing an unnecessary drama. When they finally left for a day trip, my intuition screamed at me to do something. I drove at speed to the hospital. By the time I ran through the doors of casualty Callan was unconscious and needed to be resuscitated. He could have died and I learned that day that no matter what, I needed to trust myself – regardless of how much scorn I was facing. The more we do this, the more our kids will learn by proxy how to do it for themselves.

Exercise: Body Talk

Sit with your child just before they go to sleep, or when they have woken up – this is a good time because they should be more relaxed. Ask them to imagine that their body can talk to them. Ask them to listen and see if any part of their body has something that it wants to share. (Children who experience their world much more through the physical will find this easier but any child can master it.) If they do have a pain or place that feels tight or funny, then get them to chat to that part of their body and ask it what it needs to feel better. Explain to them that their body talks to them all the time, it just uses sensation to get their attention. Tell them every time they have a feeling in their body they can talk to it and it can tell them how to be happy and healthy.

Intuitive Diagnosis

Children who use their intuition in this way can often clearly see if someone is sick or is going to become so. Often they will ask the person what's wrong with them when there are no visible signs of illness. This talent stands out because children don't seem to become fully aware of it until the age of about twelve or older. Most parents have probably had the experience of lying on the sofa with the flu, feeling like death, and the kids are running around playing at full tilt, completely oblivious. Not so for mini healing intuitives. Commonly, children who use healing intuition know from a young age that they want to make people or animals better for a living when they grow up, and a lot of their imaginative play will be around this. Often they will have an extreme fascination around the subject of health and bodies and how they work. Most importantly they have a deep understanding that all healing is possible from within, rather than through medical intervention. If you talk to older children they will often describe this knowing as remembering – the uncovering of knowledge that they once knew before.

"I learn Reiki and Thomas, my son who was four, told me he had a headache and asked me to put my hands on his head. Then he told me that was enough, took my hands off, turned over and went to sleep. I was just blown away."
- *Thomas' mum, Debbie*

"When I was 18, I spent a morning in an operating theatre as part of my University course. I stood there thinking, 'This is so barbaric. Don't they know that you can make people well without cutting them open? You just direct light at them'. Then I thought – this is the really weird bit – 'They do it differently where I come from.' "
- *Lawrence, now a doctor*

What Lawrence was observing is actually not so weird. He was probably a healer in a previous life – often healers practice their arts over many incarnations. Also the daily miracle of the body getting sick then well, is, when you really think about it, mind blowing. As a nurse I was fascinated by why some people got ill and some didn't. Healing, like intuition, comes from beyond us – it is, as all good health professionals will attest, a mystery. Despite all our scientific knowledge, we don't know what causes the body to heal. The positive side to this mystery is that more and more we are looking within ourselves for the secret to healing. If your child shows this super-sense then teach them about the body and let them explore it through books and games. Teach them about chakras and auras. If they do get an intuitive 'aha' about the onset of illness in themselves or another then follow through with some preventative action. This might be as simple as getting some more rest or a change in diet.

Holistic Intuitive

Our children are growing up at a time where there are radically changing attitudes to health care. In Australia, our kids are just as likely to visit an alternative health practitioner as they are their GP.*
The days when we thought the doctor in the white coat could fix everything are fast disappearing. Private health care cover often now includes what was once regarded as fringe complementary medicine. We now understand that health is a complex relationship between what we think and the choices we make around our body. We now know that we need to treat more than the symptoms to get well. As we transform our approach to health, we are also becoming aware that we own a great deal of power to heal ourselves.

---

* Charlie C.L. Xue, Anthony L. Zhang, Vivian Lin, Cliff Da Costa, David F. Story, *The Journal of Alternative and Complementary Medicine*, 2007, 13(6): 643-650.

Healing Potential

Children who are very plugged into this super-sense will be able to describe a sense of healing power, or actually feel it directly in their body and/or hands. They may spontaneously do simple energetic healing on pets and friends, either by just touching or by thinking of others (distance healing). These kids can usually see or sense energetic bodies and chakras and if they are out of balance.

> *"Jemima, who is seven years old, does healing on her brother. She waits until he is asleep in the cot and then sits and holds her hands up for a few minutes, then leaves. When I first saw her do it, she explained that she was sending a hug to his ears, because they were blocked. He was actually later diagnosed as having chronic glue ear. Jemima told us when she was three she wanted to be a nurse when she grew up and she hasn't changed her mind."*
> *- Jemima's mum, Rani*

If your child does show their intuition in this way, it's important to teach them how to keep their own energy from becoming depleted. Get them to imagine they have an energy-o-meter on their chest. Tell them to check it every week and if it gets too low then explain they need to download some more energy. All they have to do is ask for the energy to flow into them from the universal generator while they sleep!

Exercise: Healing Light Sabres

Let them have fun sending energy to people or objects. Get them to close their eyes and imagine the energy flowing like a fast river of light from their hands. They can imagine them as healing light sabres. See if they can feel the energy in their hands as they send it. Now swap and send it to them this time. See if they can feel where you are directing it. Explain this energy can go anywhere in the body – wherever it's needed – and it will always make them feel good.

Intuitive Hot Spot: Intuition and Illness

Children who have experienced illness, especially if it has been severe or even life-threatening, often awaken into, or deepen, their intuition. Illness is often a gateway for intuitive growth. This makes sense if you consider the body as the voice of the soul. Many holistic practitioners teach that illness is the physical manifestation of our emotional or spiritual issues. Through the process of becoming sick and getting well we are clearing through deeper issues, and this opens the space for greater levels of intuition. Also, when we are sick we are very vulnerable and therefore more open. If your child has gone through a recent crisis of health, keep an eye out for a bump-up in their super-senses.

Guided Visualisation: Healing Intuition
The Mermaid's Tail

Close your eyes. You are out on the sea on a blue and white boat. The sails flap in the wind as you dash over the white-tipped waves. The sun is shining and the sea is deep blue. Suddenly a pod of dolphins appears at the front of the boat. They are leaping and diving under the bow – it's like they're trying to get your attention. They are so close you can see their shiny skin. You can feel the radar they are pulsing out from their bodies. You get the sense they want you to follow them because someone needs help. You turn the wheel of the boat and sail with them as they surf the waves just in front of you. When you get close to an island you moor the boat and the dolphins click at you until you understand they want you to hop in. The water is so clear you can see the sand all the way at the bottom and rainbow coloured fish swimming in the depths. You jump into the warm tropical water knowing that the dolphins will keep you safe and you hold on to their fins as they speed you towards a deserted island beach. The dolphins wave their tails goodbye and you wade onto shore. The white sand feels warm beneath your toes. In the distance you can hear someone sighing. You walk up towards the rocks and there is a long red-haired mermaid. Her tail is iridescent with emerald green and silver. She is so beautiful but she looks sad. She sneezes and explains she has a croaky throat and has lost her siren song. You say you will look for it, so you set off across the beach and when you get to the middle of the island, you listen to your heart and it tells you that the song is right in front of you. You look down and see a big conch shell. When you pick it up you can hear the sound of the mermaid singing. You run back to the mermaid on the rocks and give her the shell. She is so pleased, says thank you and stops sneezing immediately. She swims you back to your boat as fast as a fish through the warm sea and then sings to you as you sail back home. You can open your eyes now and remember, you can listen to your heart whenever you need help.

Chapter 9
Intuitive Communicators

This is the information super-sense. In this chapter we'll explore some of the possibilities available to kids who use this type of intuition.

Extraordinary Communication

Kids who have this intuitive ability often know what the next big thing will be and are intrigued by anything new. They can be slow to start speaking (so was Einstein!) but when they get language under their belts they will range from chatty to being able to talk under water! These kids can be incredibly social and love connecting with people and bringing people together, often from a wide variety of backgrounds. As adults they will gravitate towards working in communication whether it be through telecommunications, publishing, advertising, media, the Internet or language. They will always be involved in cutting edge or pioneer projects; anything that pushes the limits of what is currently possible. In this way they are trendsetters in whatever area they choose to work in. They are information guzzlers and disseminators, and can be comfortable from a young age with teaching or speaking to large groups. Often they are child actors or performers. They have an intuitive ability to plug into the global, national and community vibe, to sense what's current and what's about to be. They have their intuitive finger on the zeitgeist pulse and are always just ahead of their time.

Often frustrated and impatient by the slowness of our earthbound ways of contact, these kids will think and talk at the speed of light. These super-sense kids want to break down the boundaries of what's possible in communication and are therefore not really that freaked out when they use their intuition to speak to people who have left their bodies as if they were alive, talk to spirits, ascended masters, fairies, angels and guides easily and communicate messages to others from these beings. They are also often very talented at telling astonishing stories of magical worlds which delight and entertain.

These kids have a lot in common with super-audio intuitives and the two super-senses often run in tandem. However, super communicators have a slightly different flavour. They tend to have more lively personalities and while they may hear in a super-sense way, their real strength is in transmitting and communicating information.

"My ten-year-old daughter is constantly in contact with her sister who died four years ago. She is always singing and giggling with her — even in her sleep! She also loves to talk to fairies and other magical beings — it's pretty non-stop in our house."
- Ania's mum, Trudy

If your child is one of these mercurial beings here are a few things you can do to keep them on track:

• Be very sensitive with what you say to them. These kids can have a thin skin when it comes to communicating. Be careful not to wound with words.

• Teach them patience — help them understand that not everyone can keep up with them or do what they do.

• Get them to respect the power of words. Remember the saying, 'The pen is mightier than the sword'? Explain that words can change the world and they need to choose and use them carefully.

• Get them to slow down occasionally. Help them understand they can't do everything all the time. Show them that if new projects are to succeed they need follow-through and perseverance.

• Teach them to meditate.

If you want to fast track your child's connection to this type of intuition, then support them in speaking their own truth. If children know they can speak up in safety then they will grow in self-confidence and their intuition will grow in parallel. Every great communicator has this as their foundation. Explain to them that intuition can come through what we say to others and what is said to us so it's good to listen carefully to both. Finally, if they say something wise, point it out to them.

Meditation for Minis

This is a fabulous way to teach your child the easy way to inner calm. However, if you're a busy mum or dad, the words 'meditation' and 'kids' might seem mutually exclusive. Especially if the thought of getting your child to sit quietly <u>and</u> still for more than a nanosecond seems like an impossible dream. When your home is packed with noisy toddlers and a mountain of ironing, creating a sacred space and tapping into deep peace might feel like a bit of a stretch. But the good news is that meditation is simple and free and you can do it anywhere.

And it's not difficult because kids are natural meditators and teaching them how to take time out, however briefly, in a world that is often chaotic and pressurised is one of the greatest life tools you give them. So, for a more peaceful prodigy try these four short meditations for minis:

Mindful Meditation
One of the most common misconceptions about meditation is that you have to be in silence for long periods of time. The real meaning of meditation is to bring your total awareness to whatever you are doing. Children do this beautifully when they are absorbed in something they love. They automatically bring their full attention to their activity. Doing a 'mindful

meditation' with your child is an extension of this.

Choose a project to do with your child – it can be anything from peeling potatoes to planting seeds. Engage them in it fully and really bring their awareness to all that's involved in it, the choices that are being made, how it feels and smells, and what it looks like. As they focus on these things they will become fully present in the experience and what is normally routine can become magical.

Moving Meditation

Not all meditation needs to be about stillness. Children love to be dynamic and active meditation is great for them. Again, the purpose of doing a moving meditation is to get them to be really aware of what they are doing – drawing their attention to how their body feels and how it makes them feel to move in that way. After doing this many children find it easier to play independently and in a more peaceful way.

Find a safe space, indoors or outside, where you and your child can move your bodies. Put on some music. It can be fun to experiment with different styles. Just do whatever feels good for both of you. It can be helpful to talk to them afterwards about what it felt like.

Nature Meditation

Being in nature is a meditation in itself. The sounds of birds, waves and trees or the silence of open spaces are deeply soothing for children.

Take your child into the garden or a park or down to the beach. Spend some time really looking at the flowers or lying down staring at the sky. Really take in the detail of a shell or a stone and let your child feel the wonder of exploring the natural world.

Guided Meditation

Kids love guided visualisations and they are a fabulous way of getting children to really be still and listen. Guided visualisations also stimulate their visual imaginations and help to increase their attention span.

Buy a book or CD or make your own magical meditation on tape. You can play it in the car or read it at bedtime for a deeper sleep.

Meditation is known to boost immune function, reduce stress levels and help centre us emotionally. It's also easily one of the best ways to boost your child's intuition. Fifteen minutes of meditation is also believed to be the equivalent of two hours sleep. If you want to do meditations with your little ones then try doing them together – that way you both get the benefit. Remember to make it fun for the kids; experiment with it and vary how you do it. You'll get the most benefits if you practise it regularly – ideally make time every day even if it's just for five to ten minutes.

Guided Visualisation – Super Communication

Find a safe space and close your eyes. Imagine you are standing outside an elevator. You climb in and it asks you to hold on. It zooms so fast you're not sure whether you are going up or falling down! When it stops the doors open and as you step out the elevator disappears. You are in a big room. It's white everywhere and there's no ceiling. You can see out to the stars and the dark blue sky. In the middle of the floor is a glass wardrobe. Inside it hangs a single enchanted cloak. On it are sewn silver and gold jewelled dragonflies. You take it out – it's feather light and you twirl it around. As you are spinning a magic scooter flies in where the ceiling should be and asks you to jump on. You hang onto the cloak as the scooter whisks you across oceans and icebergs and rainforests. Finally you land at the front of the biggest tower you have ever seen. You buzz the holographic entry phone and you are tele-transported to the great hall. In one half of the room it's snowing, in the other the sun is shining like mid-summer. In the middle is a powerful sorceress. You know that because she tells you when you arrive! She is very beautiful. Her hair is black on one side and blonde on the other. Her dress is divided right down the middle into dark and light. She says she has been searching everywhere for her cloak and asks you if you would help her find it. It's very special she says, it helps all the people across the world understand each other and without it she can't make her harmony spells. You hold out the dragonfly cloak and ask her if this is the one she is looking for. Delighted, she grabs it and throws it around her shoulders. The jewels flash in all directions like lasers. The sorceress thanks you and gives you a light pendant. It glows like a blue moon. She explains that when you wear it you can talk to anyone and understand everything. You slip it on and it's true – you can speak snowflake and sunbeam and star language. The whole universe is talking to you and you are talking back. The sorceress says it's been a pleasure but she's got visitors from 10 dimensions arriving for tea, so she asks if you wouldn't mind seeing yourself out. You smile and wave and whistle to the scooter, and it speeds you out the window and back to the bottom of the elevator. What an adventure! And remember you can put the pendant on anytime you like.

Chapter 10
Staying Grounded

In my experience, there are no barriers between any of the super-senses. While a child may have a preference or special gift in one area, if they try, they can usually use the other super-senses too. They may add more to their repertoire as they get older or expand in the area they have the strongest feel for.

Intuitive Labelling

While I've used terms in this book like 'sensory gifted' to describe children who use their intuition easily, I want to say that I feel strongly that it's a mistake to label children in any way and especially in regard to their intuition. Defining a child with a label immediately limits them. It puts them in a box and boxes have boundaries and I don't know about you but I don't want to put boundaries on my child. Intuition as far as I have explored it has no limits or restriction – that's part of its divine beauty – so I think it's a mistake to restrict our kids in relation to it. If the terms are useful, that's great, but that's all they are. Our children are so much bigger than any of the labels we can assign to them to describe their behaviour and special abilities.

Sometimes when their intuition really wants to get their attention, it can transmit through a variety of senses at one time. The result can be a show-stopping experience. One of the most intense I've had was when I was asking for guidance about whether or not I should apply to move to Australia from the UK. My chances for a long-term visa looked slim but I felt very drawn to live there. I was in the Strand in London and popped into an Australian shop for ex-pats there.

"As I walked into the shop, I saw in front of me a huge colour photo of Uluru (Ayers Rock), the most sacred aboriginal site in Australia — a place I had visited earlier that year and which had profoundly affected me. In the same instant, I heard the haunting, indigenous music that was playing in the store. Suddenly as I entered, everything around me started to change. I was moving at normal speed but the people in the shop were all in slow motion. They were talking but the sound was distorted and muted. I walked around past everyone but it was as if they couldn't see me. The music was so loud and resonating so powerfully I could see its vibrations moving through the store. The picture on the walls of rainforest and desert and cities, seemed to be alive. Simultaneously I was flooded with an intense feeling of peace and joy, and a deep knowing that this was the right destination for me. As I approached the cash desk everything snapped back into real time and I looked around astonished that no one else had noticed the change. The imprint on me was indelible. I knew where I was headed and the exhilaration of these few moments stayed with me through the challenge of my visa application — which against the odds, was successful!"

Experiencing the whole intuitive shebang like that is quite rare but every child that uses their intuition can experience something similar. The best way to approach it is to have no expectations about how it will pan out for them. However they evolve intuitively is fine. No super-sense is better than another, although some are more common. What we as parents can do, is recognise where our children's strengths lie, encourage them to experiment and help them make sense of what they are experiencing. We can also help them integrate if their sensory giftedness goes up a notch. This is very important because children who use their intuition a great deal can often have trouble staying grounded. When they start to un-ground they begin to lose part of their connection with their body, their sense of self or their surroundings, so that they might have a sense of being a little separate, cut off or cut loose.

Children can find it very hard to articulate what this is like but commonly they will feel and appear a bit out of balance; off kilter somehow. This is more often the case for a child who easily accesses their intuition but it's also an issue for those who are developing their intuitive skills. It can happen at any age and frequently goes hand in hand with an expansion of their intuitive self. While any child can be affected, children who would be regarded as more sensitive, either emotionally, physically or intuitively will tend to have a bigger reaction. It's crucial to underline that this is <u>not</u> a bad or dangerous thing. It's just the same as if a child does too much training in sport or too much studying. Plugging into intuition means connecting with a lot of positive energy and sometimes, there can be a bit of overload – especially for small bodies and systems that are very dynamic in their own right. Think of it as a signpost that your child needs to pace themselves, or have a bit more support around their intuition. If a child starts to disconnect then it's increasingly unlikely that they will be able to access their inner wisdom and ultimately, without attention, they can become very blocked.

An ungrounded child is actually a great opportunity, because in helping them come back in balance, we teach them how to ground themselves in the future. It's very important then, when we are working around our kids intuition, that we keep an eye out for signs that our child needs to come back to centre.

Trouble-shooting – Signs that a child is not grounded:

• They lack concentration and seem distracted or restless.
• When they listen they don't absorb what's being said to them.
• They seem tired and lack energy regardless of how much sleep they have.
• They can find it hard to go to sleep and wake early or often.
• They can seem off balance – easily upset or irritable, with wild mood swings.
• They find it harder to cope with new situations than they would normally.

• Their appetite can drop or they may get very picky with their food.
• They might seem nervous, edgy or a bit strung out.

In most cases these symptoms will be very subtle and can be easily confused with a kid having an 'off' day or a pre-teen any day! If you have any concerns, get them checked out by a health professional. However if you're confident that there are no other underlying causes then observe and see if there's a pattern. Normally on closer inspection you will reveal a relationship between intuitive bursts and a period of ungrounded behaviour.

How to deal with it:

• Take action to slow them down. Have a quiet weekend at home with minimal amounts of TV and computer.
• Do a switching off exercise with them, where they visualise hitting a 'snooze button' so they can have a break from the flow of intuitive information.
• Help them relax by letting them have a nap, a warm bath, a slow walk or short meditation/visualisation.
• Nurture them by creating some one-on-one space with them, even if it's just for a short time. Sit and play together – laugh, have fun.
• Make sure they eat nourishing foods and avoid sugar and additives.
• Take them out into nature, to the park, especially beside water or to play at the beach.
• Let them take comfort in favourite things – books, movies, toys – whatever makes them feel safe.
• Encourage them to play, preferably outside, with friends they interact easily with.

If your child's intuition is opening up at a rapid rate, you may have to do some of this every day. Children recover very quickly, so you should see a quick improvement in a short time – just keep it going until you feel they're back to their version of 'normal'.

Exercise: The Grounding Tree

Close your eyes, lie on the floor and imagine that you are a tree growing into the ground. You are big and strong with a solid wide trunk and branches that stretch into the sky. Imagine that your chest and stomach and torso and legs are all part of the wise old tree. Feel how invincible that feels. Now feel your feet on the ground and imagine that they are planted in the earth. Now see all the powerful roots that grow deep in the ground holding you like a rock, steady and sure. See them spreading down from your feet going down, down into the ground. Everything that you need comes through these roots. There are hundreds of them, thick and steadfast. Feel the soil all around them holding them unmoveable in the earth. Mighty roots, rugged trunk, strong branches. Coming from the earth and stretching into the sky. Feel your strength. When you're ready you can open your eyes and every time you see a tree, you will remember how strong you can be.

Chapter 11
Shutdown

For many Gen I's, as their sensory gifts increase and as they move through different points of development, they will have new challenges to face. The way intuitive kids experience their world can be intense and overwhelming and it can be difficult for them to process this. As they get a bit older they may feel separate, different or isolated from their peers, family or community. Most young Gen I's don't consider their abilities to be anything special – since it's natural for them and has always been that way, they don't question it. It's only as they begin to compare themselves, with say, an older generation with different attitudes, that there can be a growing or sudden awareness that they experience the world in a very different way. For some children this can be a shocking and unsettling revelation and needs to be handled sensitively.

This can be even more difficult if the child is in a community that does not understand, recognise or feel comfortable with these gifts. They can be misunderstood, thought of as 'weird', and there may be the temptation to stamp out their differences and make them fit in somehow. A major issue for Gen I's and their carers is that intuitive children can create fear in others because they are more easily able to do what is considered unusual or what has, in the past, been linked to the 'supernatural'. Despite the fact that we live in a modern, sophisticated age, Gen I's can still come up against a lot of prejudice around their sensory gifts. It's essential that parents equip their children to deal with this and give them practical ways to protect themselves from the fear of others. Historically, having 'supernatural' powers or being intuitive has got a very bad rap. In the past, this lack of understanding was usually tied to a lot of old belief systems and superstitions. It's not that long ago – around a few hundred years ago – that being a mystic or having an affinity with nature meant persecution or death. Men and women – an astonishing five million of them – were hunted as witches and burned for three centuries. That's a lot of negativity! While we thankfully live in more enlightened times there is still a hangover that we all carry to some extent from these violent days. While more positive representations are coming through, our culture is still saturated with stereotypical stories, in movies and books, that link sensory giftedness to evil. Often this is portrayed as a dark side or as outside forces beyond our control. The nasty witch, the scary fortune-teller, and the wicked seer are still deep in our consciousness with all their limiting associations.

As caregivers of these super-sense children, what we most want to avoid is the worst-case scenario where an intuitive child is made to feel guilty or ashamed, or is ridiculed for their gifts, or if what they can do is ignored or denied. Children who are made to feel that who they are is wrong come into great conflict with themselves. They often feel that to receive the love and acceptance they crave from their parents and carers, they have to reject a part of them that feels as natural as breathing. Children in this situation will make themselves wrong, shut down their intuition and probably stop accessing that part of themselves altogether. They stop trusting themselves and come to believe that they are not acceptable or loveable just as they are. Children are programmed, as a survival mechanism, to always believe that their parents or carers version of the truth is the correct one, even if at a deep level they sense there is something not quite right with what they are being told. If this conflict occurs, the most likely outcome is that they will abandon their intuition in order to fit in.

Alternatively, if they don't stop tuning into their sensory gifts they may continue using their intuition but it will go underground. The child will no longer share his or her experiences and it will become something that is secret. If this happens they may feel that what they are doing is somehow 'wrong' but not want to stop. Either way, if an intuitive child does not feel safe or supported, or feels they are strange or separate because of what they experience, they will, in some way, start to shut down their intuitive gifts.

Shutdown

Shutdown can be gradual or sudden, partial or total. While it's nearly always temporary, it can sometimes take many years for their intuition to start to open fully again. In extreme situations a Gen I kid may close the lid on their intuition for the rest of their lives. Sadly this is not all that rare, but it can be prevented in most cases. The point to keep in mind is that virtually all sensory gifted children will at some point, in their journey towards adulthood, experience shutdown to some extent. Our job as carers is to be able to recognise it and help to create an environment where it can be reversed.

If you come to realise that you may have caused your child to shut down, don't worry, the damage can be healed – though it may take some time. During the recovery process, older children may no longer want to speak to their parents but rather find someone else they trust. This can be challenging but it's important to respect the child's right to confide in whoever they feel comfortable with.

Signs that your Gen I kid has shutdown their intuition can be overt or subtle. In school age children it may show itself in their refusing suddenly to talk about topics that they previously chatted about quite freely. Or you might witness irritation or avoidance if you bring up the subject. In younger children you may observe that they no longer play certain games, stop doing a favourite activity or seem to lose interest or confidence in something they once really enjoyed. There may be a sense that the child is somehow sad, angry or lost; a feeling that they have in some way become disconnected from themselves. In extreme cases shutdown can lead to physical illness, depression and suicidal thoughts.

"Rowan got teased by his home-teacher when he shared about how he talked to Angels. He was upset at first and then went very quiet. I think it was a shock to him that not everyone believed him. Since then he's stopped mentioning

them. I tried to talk to him but he just got embarrassed and cranky so I left it."

- Lorraine, mum of Rowan, aged seven and a half

Shutdown can also happen even if you are very cool about your Gen I kid's intuitive gifts, because there may be times, when they feel like the whole intuitive thing is in the 'too hard' basket. Obviously if the child is older and can talk about it, then it's easier to tackle. If it's a younger child or one who doesn't like to share, the best measure of how they're coping with their sensory gifts is their behaviour. If they are happy, sleeping and eating well, playing comfortably with other children and their siblings, then it's pretty likely they are in harmony with their intuitive side. If your child is withdrawn, having nightmares, showing continual bad behaviour or seems unduly anxious or scared then, firstly, get them checked out by a sympathetic health specialist and secondly, see if they've become swamped by their intuitive powers.

Sometimes kids shut down their intuition because of external factors that are not directly related to their super-senses. Abuse, divorce or family break-up, moving house or school, bullying at home or in the playground or exposure to scary stories or movies are usually the primary causes in these cases. They may react more acutely because of their heightened sensitivity, but the sensitivity itself is not the catalyst.

However shutdown happens, know that intuition can always be rediscovered and that for a Gen I, a temporary closing up of the intuitive shop can be a way of slowing things down and learning their boundaries, how to survive and how to be more in control of their gift.

"When I was a young teenager my sensory gifts, as well as my hormones, were running out of control, my intuition was incredibly powerful and, because of my lack of knowledge about how to channel it, very chaotic. Every day I had insight into future events – I saw my father have a car accident an hour before he did – I could sense my dead mother around the house, I had no one to talk to, I was being bullied at school and I was incredibly scared. On a couple of occasions I took a risk to share with a teacher and an adult friend who were both related to the religious community I was brought up in. No one really

seemed to know what to do with me. The message was the same — I was just very imaginative and it would go away if I stopped thinking about it. Given that I felt my whole world was spinning off its axis, this was like putting a band-aid on a severed arm. I remember very clearly the moment I decided to shut everything down. I didn't feel safe and no one believed my truth. I pictured myself gathering all the energy I could summon up and trapping it all behind this energetic brick wall I built around it. I put a huge sign on the front, 'Do Not Open'. It stayed that way for 15 years." *(Author)*

Coming Out

Even if you are completely supportive of your child in every way, there may come a time when they share or show their intuition outside of their immediate family, either at school or with friends and they are met with a less than positive reaction. It can be hard to get the right balance between an open, trusting child who is happy to share and one who knows they need to make a call on who they should trust with their intuitive insights. There are no fixed guidelines on this, it will always depend on the individual situation at hand. Explain that it's a great idea to talk to people in their inner circle about what they experience but wise to keep quiet with the rest. If they're not sure, suggest they check with their intuition and with you first.

Ultimately the best way to protect your child from others' negative conditioning is to bullet-proof their self-esteem. If your child knows they're alright regardless of what anyone thinks or says then you have a world-beater on your hands. The five top ways to boost self-esteem around intuition are:

1. Accept your child's ability.
2. Praise them for using it positively.
3. Encourage them to use their intuition.
4. If it's being used creatively, allow it free expression.
5. Give them bucket-loads of reassurance.

Intuition — NO WAY!

Very occasionally there will be a child who, for no obvious reason, will choose not to have anything to do with their own intuition. They will reject forcibly any ideas or suggestions made to them in that area. This can be baffling for parents who are keen to encourage their children in this way, especially if there has been no negative experience in their past to explain their resistance. Children like this will often show very strong reactions of fear and anger if you persist. If this is a familiar scenario in your household then the best way forward is to back off! You can still nurture your child's intuition by creating a positive environment for it but leave the rest alone. If you push this, you will end up alienating your child, possibly for good. Usually it helps to take a bigger picture approach in this situation and assume that there are reasons, as yet unknown, why it's not a good idea for them to open up their intuition at this point. The reasons I have come across for this are:

a. Their intuition is meant to/going to open suddenly, all at once during a watershed point in their lives.

b. The child has too many other issues in their life to cope with it, such as parents separating or family trauma.

c. They have very powerful, intuitive gifts and they need to be more mature to cope with them.

d. For reasons that are important to their soul development, they have made the decision not to use this part of themselves for a part or all of their lifetime. The best example I can give of this was a teenage girl I once met who had been a healer in many previous lifetimes, but had made the choice to have a break from it this time, so she could experience other ways of being. When I spoke to her she knew she had the ability to heal but didn't want to go there.

e. They had a bad experience around this issue in a past life and have not healed it yet.

Whatever the mitigating circumstances, the important thing is to honour the child's decision and not to do anything which pushes them further in the opposite direction. Interestingly while I have met many adults who are sad that they shut down their intuition because of fear or lack of support, I've never met an adult who wished they had forced their intuition to open earlier. It seems very clear that if the timing isn't right then it's best to leave well alone.

Chapter 12
Intuitive Education

One of the most common comments I get from parents of Gen I kids is that they don't fit in very well into mainstream education. There are a couple of good reasons for this. Firstly, in general, public education is not set up to deal with intuitive kids. Despite many excellent teachers working very hard, most experience gained at school is likely to crush intuition rather than help it to grow. Secondly, intuitive children normally find their ways of being to be in conflict with conventional educational institutions. These are kids who tend to question or challenge the status quo, rather than flow with it and highly intuitive kids can have challenges with concentrating and behaviour.

So what to do? Well, obviously our kids must go to school, but until intuitive studies become part of the national curriculum or alternative forms of education exist to support more intuitive ways of learning we need to choose their schools carefully. Given they will spend more time at school and with their teachers than they do with their parents or primary care givers, choosing a school which will support and nurture our kids intuitively is possibly one of the most important choices we can make as parents. In reality, many parents have very limited choices when it comes to education because of what's available locally or what they can afford financially.

However with a bit of research you can maximise your options:

• Do the legwork – ask other parents and check out the schools in the area personally. The best way to get a good sense of a school's vibe is to walk around it. In general, smaller schools with small class sizes are better.

• Speak to teachers at the school. A school is only as good as the people who work in it. The kind of relationship a child has with their teacher can make or break their year. If you can find a teacher who is sympathetic to the intuitive side of life – even better!

• Choose a school which is good match for your child's personality. I have two sons but because of their very different personalities I had to choose a school that could accommodate both their academic needs and interests. If your child has an artistic focus or a science base or is sport mad, find a school which will cater for their particular passion.

• Consider Steiner, Montessori and other independent schools which have a philosophy that supports religious and cultural diversity and difference. This is especially important if you have a child who falls into the sensory gifted bracket. There are usually large waiting lists for places at these schools, so get your child's name down early. If you are sending a child to a school which teaches within a particular religious framework, check if it can find space within that to accommodate your child's burgeoning abilities.

If your child is miserable at school, talk to their teacher and the principal. If you don't see any improvement after that then you may have to re-think your choices. Moving schools can be an upheaval but leaving them where they are can lead to irreparable trauma if they are unhappy.

"Liam, 10, is not doing well at his school. He doesn't fit in to the public system – he finds it hard to sit still and concentrate and he is very questioning of authority. He is very wise, beyond his years, and he wants to be treated as an equal rather than just a kid. It's full on. He spends recess talking with his friends about chakras and healing. He even does mini–readings for people – they're very popular! They have a little group but it's not enough. I've got his name down for a great place – it's government funded. The emphasis is

on the children learning through their own exploration. There's a lot more freedom."

- Liam's mum, Siobhan

Tools of the Trade

Letting children use tools of divination, such as runes or tarot, and giving readings needs to be approached with caution. Often traditional decks require an adult sensibility. There is an ever increasing number of wisdom cards targeted specifically at children, which is great. If they are drawn to them then let them explore but it's important to reinforce that their intuition is always more accurate and powerful than any external guidance. The emphasis for younger children should be to let them play and make mistakes without any pressure. Parents of children who are sensory gifted must be wary of letting their child be exploited. The best analogy I can give here is of child actors. They are always supervised on set and their working conditions are exceptionally regulated. So, protect your child's intuitive abilities in the same way.

Discipline and your Intuitive Child

Liam's story raises an important issue around freedom and discipline. Many intuitive children struggle with traditional modes of parenting and authority. Allowing your child to live according to their deep impulses and to be entirely authentic is a very big challenge for parents. It also asks the question, how do we reel-in our intuitive kids while still respecting them and what they do? There might seem to be an inherent contradiction in the idea that a child can be acting on their own intuition and at the same time, also behaving as we would like them to. The fear that we will end up with out of control kids because we allowed them to follow their inner guidance is very real for many mums and dads. The truth is that raising intuitive children does ask us to take a look at how we discipline our kids and perhaps re-think. We've left behind the days where children just had to do what their parents decided – thank goodness. Yet we still want to give our children the security of strong boundaries, mutual respect and co-operation at home.

There's no question that children who regularly tap into their intuition are going to be more questioning, more able to ask for what they want and more likely to argue their case. It's important here to separate challenge from downright naughtiness. All kids are badly behaved at some point – actually, it's their right. Learning not to be destructive, hurtful or selfish is part of growing up. Children must test limits to work out what's acceptable and it's our job to guide them. However sometimes it's not naughtiness, it's questioning. Intuition inevitably encourages individualism, a new way of looking at things and the courage to try new things. Despite our fears, living an intuitive life will give a child a greater, not lesser responsibility for the self. It encourages them to understand that they are connected and therefore, they need to give consideration to others when it comes to taking action and making choices. As children move deeper into their intuitive selves their behaviour will reflect values of kindness, compassion and personal accountability. There's no quick fix for getting there though. Parenting intuitive children takes constant negotiation and it's something I believe this generation of parents is exploring every day. The reality is that there will be times where our kids' intuition may be telling them something that is in direct opposition to what we may have taught them, as the case of Jo, aged ten, highlights:

"Dad was late home and I didn't know why. As I cleared up in the kitchen, I imagined a policeman came to our door. I knew it wasn't real, but it was just like he was there. He explained that the reason Dad was delayed was because he had been in a car accident but that he wasn't hurt. For some reason I felt angry and upset at the policeman and I shouted at him to go away. I knew it didn't make sense that I should be mad at him when he was trying to help but that's what I felt. It was so strong, I started to cry."
- Jo, aged 10

When Jo's father finally arrived he explained a car had run into the back of his car on his way home. There was no injury but the car was damaged.

When police arrived at the scene, it turned out the driver was himself an off-duty police officer and had been drinking. Reluctant to book a colleague more senior than themselves, they made Jo's father take a breath test and tried to persuade him to take responsibility for the incident. Despite the intimidation Jo's father stood his ground and the officer was finally charged.

Jo's vision shows the importance of teaching our children to trust what they see and feel, even if it goes against conventional wisdom. Jo had been taught to trust police as authority figures and to call them if she was in trouble. Yet in this instance her intuition was telling her to beware. Our children's sensory gifts are there to guide them and keep them safe and they need to be respected. This offered Jo a great opportunity to learn that while it's wonderful to put faith in an institution or person, that should be superseded by her own insight. She learnt that her own super-sight would never let her down and that it was safe to trust it despite external signs to the contrary.

If we do get into conflict with our children on this issue, we need to stay open and keep working at it. The most important thing about discipline is to do it consciously. If you're thinking about these issues and talking about them, then you can't do better than that – even if you do make a wrong call occasionally. We all make mistakes, but in the words of childcare expert Robin Barker in her book 'Baby Love', "it's better to do the wrong thing in love than the right thing without love". And it goes without saying that we need to keep checking in that we are walking our talk! Children learn the most by copying what their parents do – not what they say!! If you think you could be handling this issue better with your child but are not sure how – consult with your own intuition!

Intuition and Personal Beliefs

There are a number of reasons that parents might want to bypass the whole intuition issue. They may think it's all a bit bogus or they totally believe in it but don't want to unduly influence their children. I love it that parents have an increasing respect for their children's beliefs and choices and want them to have the space to explore things in their own way. However I think there is an important distinction between imposing what you believe and exposing what you believe. Part of a child's intuitive journey is to choose what works for them – something that children are naturally very good at. So it makes sense to open up information that might be helpful to them and let them pick what they feel serves them. Children also learn through trial and error. If they give something a go and it works for them then they will use it again – if it doesn't they will soon let you know. So don't be afraid to share your own beliefs with your children. Let them know how you see the world so they can decide for themselves what works for them and what doesn't.

"I'm on my own journey with this stuff but I haven't wanted to impose my beliefs. But looking back I feel like I did my kids a bit of a disfavour. I wish now I had gone with the flow."
- Amanda

"I was brought up in a very religious family and I've spent most of my adult life trying to release myself from all the conditioning. I now consider myself a deeply spiritual person but avoid sharing it with my children for fear I'll damage them by being too dogmatic. At the same time I feel like I'm letting them down... What I realise is that it's not what I share, it's the way I share it that counts. If I do it in a spirit of openness and enquiry then they can make up their own minds about it."
- Antonella

Alternatively, if you've never had an interest in this area before then you might feel totally underqualified to help your children with intuition and have no idea where to start.

"When it started to happen for my kids, I started to look for information and I found it frustrating because there wasn't anything. I looked for a book for children but I didn't really find anything where I thought, 'this is it'. There was nothing specific enough. If I did talk to people they would just look at me as if I was the strangest thing on two legs. I felt very isolated about it. I was trying to draw on my experiences but I wasn't in an open environment

about it - my husband was the biggest sceptic there is. I didn't know how to get people to talk to me.
- Debbie

Finally, it may be that a lot of the stuff around intuition comes into conflict with your personal or religious beliefs. This is a tough one; however in my experience, intuition, if we can be open to it, deepens our connection with our personal idea of God/the Goddess/Allah or whatever name you choose. Intuition takes us closer to 'all that is', not further away. Intuition is, at its core, love in action, which is about as accurate a description of God as I know. If you are struggling with the whole idea of intuition or if your child is using their intuition a lot and you are feeling overwhelmed – it's okay. Anxiety about what they can do, what you think about it and how to handle it can be very strong. There's nothing wrong with feeling unsure, confused sceptical, disapproving or resistant. What counts is what you do about it. So if you are freaking out a bit and don't know how to proceed, take some comfort from the answers to five of the most commonly asked questions by parents and carers of Gen I children:

Can their sensory gifts be removed?

No. Your Gen I child can't be fixed or changed. Your child is as unable to stop their intuition as they are their ability to smell or taste. They can shut it down but it won't disappear – even if you want it to!

Can what they do hurt or damage them?

Not at all! Intuition is always and only available for our benefit.

Is it evil?

I personally believe that there is no evil outside what we create ourselves. However I know that there can often be fears about 'dark forces' at work in sensory gifted kids. The question that ultimately has to be answered is: Are these abilities coming from a place of love? My answer is that the defining nature of intuition is its truth and integrity. It inevitably brings us closer to, not further away from, the divine within us and others.

Can they use it to hurt others?

No. All gifts need to be learned to be used responsibly and with love and this is equally true for intuitive kids. Showing Gen I's how to use their sensory gifts for everyone's advantage is part of the challenge of being their carer. Even if they do act in error with it, no serious harm can be done.

Isn't it a load of new age nonsense?

Well, I don't think so but why not give it a go and make up your own mind about it? You have nothing to lose. Regardless of how you feel about intuition, the point is if you have a Gen I kid, one way or another it has to be handled. And the bonus is that as you move towards opening up to their abilities, you automatically give permission for that part of yourself to be free – perhaps for the first time in many years.

The most important thing is to respect your child's abilities and see them, for example, in the same way as you would academic achievement. Coming to a point of acceptance about what your child can do is especially important because Gen I's are energetic sponges and will be acutely sensitive to what you – the most important person in their lives – think and feel about them. Until they come in contact with opposition they will just accept their intuition as part of who they are. If it is a big deal for you and brings up a negative reaction, especially a strong one, it can be helpful to remember that this is just conditioning – somewhere along the line you came to believe that this kind of thing was bad. Spending a little time thinking about where the source of the negativity is can be very useful. It may be that your own parents or culture attached superstition to sensory gifts. It might be a grief reaction that your child is not 'normal' and the fear that their life might be difficult or somehow unsafe as a result. Or interestingly, often when parents do a little emotional archaeology, they remember that as a child they were quite intuitive themselves. They may have been made to feel bad about it, had a negative experience or didn't have support or anyone to talk to and so, stopped using it. We often reject in others the things we cannot accept about
ourselves.

It's interesting that while researching this book, I found fathers were much less willing to admit what their kids could do with their intuition. When they did start to talk it was always the same story – that they had been very sceptical but had had to admit something was going on. Many of them told me amazing examples of their child's intuition but were still reluctant to embrace it enthusiastically. It's hardly surprising that men find intuition difficult, going as it does against the masculine construct of logic and accountability. Intuition has always been associated with the feminine; we talk about 'female intuition' after all. And there's no question it has many feminine qualities, spontaneity, creativity, power that's not aggressive, compassion, love, abundance, elusiveness, freedom – to name a few.

However there are no gender differences when it comes to intuition. Our sons have intuition too and they need support as well. Men need to reclaim their intuition, to see it as strong and essential so that they can lose the fear of owning this part of themselves. Real men are intuitive too!!

Chapter 13
Intuition & Pregnancy

Baby Intuitive

Some Gen I children will make their presence felt from an early stage which can make for an interesting nine months when you are pregnant. Growing another human being inside you and having your body and emotions running like an out of control freight train makes most 'normal' pregnancies challenging enough. However, while you are both sharing the same body, you can easily pick up on their super-sense energy and in turn they will be boosting yours. The results can be extraordinary – welcome to Generation Intuitive!

Signs that you are intuitively linked to your child are:

1. You have vivid dreams while pregnant
The quality and intensity of night and daydreaming commonly increases while you are pregnant. With Gen I babies this will be even more so. Dreams are often recurring, extremely detailed and have a strong emotional quality.

2. You have the repeated notion that you are both tapping into how the other is feeling and there seems to be a lot of synchronicity.

On many occasions you will be mirroring each other's moods and will be able to sense where the other is at.

3. You feel that your child tries hard to communicate with you.
Gen I babies will use a variety of methods to be in touch with you or get your attention – some of them quite comical, like hiccups or constant turning. Of course babies have always done these things but with Gen I's you will be aware that it's a clear communication. Apart from movements they will also send you messages which can come through as thoughts or emotions which, on inspection, you recognise as the baby's rather than your own.

> " *I worked out a system of talking to my son before he was born. I would ask a question and push my bump and a couple of seconds later he would push back in exactly the same place. I felt very connected to him in a sensory way. After he was born I felt there was still a strong link. We often mirrored each other in the positions we slept in, even at opposite ends of the house. I always woke seconds before him. Even now that he's seven he'll say to me, 'I can read your mind.' And he can!"*
> - Holly, mum to Jack, aged 7

4. Your own senses escalate while you are carrying the child.
An increase in all your senses and awareness might be experienced. Intuition, inner wisdom and even the five main senses of sight, smell, taste, touch and hearing can all become super-senses.

5. You experience amazing coincidences or phenomena while pregnant.
You are experiencing the world just as they will.

> *"I've always been aware that I've had intuition but it's developed at a rate of knots since I was pregnant with Lila - almost too fast for me. I woke up five weeks before her birth and someone was shouting her name in my ear. We looked Lila up on the internet and it has a metaphysical meaning too. Now I listen to my intuition every single day."*
> - Amanda

6. You have fears or longings that come up at different points in your pregnancy,

which may be inexplicable or irrational.
Frequently mums of Gen I children will experience emotions or anxieties
that do not seem directly related to their current pregnancy. These highly
sensory children can be a catalyst for bringing past life experiences involving
the two of you to the surface for healing.

> *"When I was pregnant with my daughter, I had so many fears and dreams
> about her arriving safely. There was no logical explanation for the way I
> felt and in a strange way it seemed that my anxieties didn't belong to me.
> Because she was breech, I went to see a healer to see if we could get her to turn
> naturally. The healer spoke to my unborn girl and she told me that I had lost
> her in childbirth in a previous life but this time everything would be fine. We
> did some healing around that original grief and the fears disappeared. She
> turned that night while I slept and I had a perfect labour and birth."*
> - Jackie, mum to Lily, aged 2

7. You have a sense that you have known this child before.
You have a strong feeling that this baby is very familiar or that you have a
deep understanding of them from the beginning.

*8. You saw flashes of light and colour or celestial beings just before you were pregnant,
at the moment of conception or in the first few days of pregnancy.*
Gen I children often come accompanied by some super-sensory fanfare.
Mums may see or feel, bursts of light, a heightened awareness of everything
around them or simply a deep knowing that they are carrying another
soul.

If you are experiencing some or all of these, then get ready to welcome
your Gen I child. Feel confident that this is all normal – even if it doesn't
feel like it! And be prepared for the possibility that all of these phenomena
get stronger as the pregnancy progresses. You can start to communicate
with your unborn child's sensory self from the moment you know you
are pregnant. Tune into them through quiet time, meditation or simply by
listening to your body. This meditation is a great way to begin a beautiful life
long intuitive relationship with your child.

Baby Love Meditation

Create some quiet time each day - quite a feat for any mum or mum to be - and sit quietly. Put your hand on your bump, relax and breathe deeply. Imagine yourself in a beautiful landscape – wherever you feel serene and safe and invite your baby to come and talk to you. If you cannot see him or her in your mind's eye, don't worry, you can get a sense of them or hear them if that works for you. Ask your child what it needs to share with you and speak freely to them of your hopes and fears. It's important to trust the messages that come through. You might get them as a sense or a feeling or a thought that pops into your head. Thank your child for sharing with you and for being who they are.

Congratulations – you've just had your first sensory contact with your Mini Gen I.

Mini Gen I's

Children can show their intuition from the time they are small babies, which can be a bit of a freak-out for parents. These bubs will seem to be more in tune and can have a powerful energy. Often they may appear to be watching or listening to things around them that we cannot see or hear. Mums especially can pick up on this but feel reluctant to say anything because they fear appearing foolish. The message here for parents is – trust your own intuition. No one knows your child like you do!

Another signal that your very young child is using their intuition is that they seem to have a strong sense of what is happening immediately around them. They can pick up how their parents or carers are feeling and what the emotional undertow is in any situation. These sensitive souls can be difficult to settle and initially need a great deal of quiet to sleep. They can often get overwrought by being out in the world and being exposed to a lot of energy. Often extremely alert children, they show a great desire to communicate even before they are at a stage of language. This alertness can show itself in a variety of ways. They might be very engaging with people around them in an intense way. They may watch very carefully what is happening around them. They might show a huge interest in the environment around them and want to interact with it or they may just feel very peaceful and centred in themselves. Super-sense babies can often seem very sympathetic; they will look at you as if they understand, especially if you are having a trying time. However it plays out and even if you can't easily explain it, you will probably have figured out that what this baby can do is exceptional.

Star Children

To help understand your child's intuitive make up and help them fulfil their special destiny it can be useful to know some basic information about their astrological profile. Your child's astrological sun sign can be part of the key to their future success and happiness and will often influence how they use their intuition. Find out their inherent astro qualities, so that you can channel your child's unique purpose.

Aries (21 March – 20 April)
Sunside: Adventurous, Fearless, Passionate
Little rams are often born early because they are in a hurry to get here! They are loud, big on energy and walk and run early. Determined to get their own way they can be demanding. Encourage their huge imagination and allow them complete self-expression. Aries children have big dreams and the energy to make them come true.
Intuitive strengths: Physical / Visual

Taurus (21 April – 21 May)
Sunside: Affectionate, Determined, Creative
Baby bulls can be born late – they like to take their own time. They welcome routine and order. Taurean children will be warm and cuddly. They crave harmony but happy or unhappy they will let you know – loudly! Obstinate

in the extreme, you can guide them towards their own great judgement. Believe they can create whatever they desire – because they can!
Intuitive strengths: Feeling/Physical

Gemini (22 May – 21 June)
Sunside: Communication, Intelligent, Curious
Gemini children are constantly inquisitive, free spirits who love to explore, adventure and experience. Their passion is to communicate, they're usually big talkers, fast learners and often highly psychic and artistic, they sometimes need help to relax. Love your Gemini child unconditionally, however unconventional – their difference will lead them to success.
Intuitive strengths: Communication/Vision

Cancer (22 June – 23 July)
Sunside: Intuitive, Open Hearted, Sensitive
Baby crabs bring with them a sense of vulnerability. Little Cancerians need to be nurtured and live in a world of thoughts and feelings. Very sensitive, they can cry a lot but they're actually very resilient and can be tough to get their own way. Swamp your Cancer child with lots of love and hugs, and the space to follow their daydreams. The castles they build in their minds can become empires when they are adults.
Intuitive strengths: Feeling/Healer

Leo (24 July – 23 August)
Sunside: Confident, Enthusiastic, Brave
Little lions are strong personalities, with huge physical energy. They like to be the centre of attention and often make a dramatic entrance into the world. Your Leo will have star quality. They often get their own way are noisy and boisterous and like to lead. If you can get them to knuckle down to hard work and cherish their tender hearts they can be champions.
Intuitive strengths: Audio/Physical

Virgo (24 August – 23 September)
Sunside: Logical, Perfectionist, Individual
Virgo children are practical, caring and considerate. They long for smooth, running, harmony. Little Virgoans are original thinkers and very analytical.

They like to work things out and are extremely observant. Harsh words wound them and they can be hard on themselves, so always be positive around them. Virgos hard work and talent means they can succeed at anything.
Intuitive strengths: Knowing/Communication

Libra (24 September – 23 October)
Sunside: Balanced, Charming, Gentle
Libran children are extremely attractive. Appealing, funny, wonderful and happy they can also be moody and award-winning sulkers! They know from birth what they do and do not like and will charm you till they get it. Libran children care what you think of them – so give them lots of praise. Their natural taste and desire to create beauty will make them a winner in life.
Intuitive strengths: Audio/Vision

Scorpio (24 October – 22 November)
Sunside: Mystical, Imaginative, Powerful
Your Scorpio child will always keep you guessing. They have a mind and destiny all of their own. Leaders who love change, they are persistent and intense and can take time to settle into routine. Their self-confidence and determination to stay on their own path should always be supported. They have big visions and the inspiration to bring them into reality.
Intuitive strengths: Vision/Healing

Sagittarius (23 November – 21 December)
Sunside: Adaptable, Optimistic, Impulsive
Little Archers are go-getters who love adventure. They are rebellious and freedom is very important to them. They can take change and won't complain too loudly – just don't cramp their style. Saggs are big explorers, who often develop early. For your little Archer to do well, love them with an open mind and they will be an unstoppable force.
Intuitive strengths: Physical/Communication

Capricorn (22 December – 20 January)
Sunside: Honest, Reliable, Caring
Kid goats are serious and often feel like old souls. They love routine and

are good with boundaries. Being accepted or rejected is very important to them. Often slow to walk or talk, when they do achieve they like a lot of praise. Help them to be spontaneous and appreciate loudly their good traits and their natural wisdom will take them to greatness.

Intuitive strengths: Knowing/Audio

Aquarius (21 January – 19 February)
Sunside: Original, Tolerant, Inventive

With this child expect variety. Aquarian children are free thinkers and highly individual. For parents the art to learn is compromise. Doing things their way is not a phase but a way of life and this is what leads them to success. Aquarians are magical children who will challenge you, and the status quo, and can bring in positive change and new ways of being.

Intuitive strengths: Healing/Knowing

Pisces (20 February – 20 March)
Sunside: Compassionate, Graceful, Understanding

Little fish are delicate souls, often highly psychic. They like warmth and tenderness. Security is the cornerstone of their world and small Pisceans' sensitivity will pick up on any disharmony at home. These dreamy children are intuitive and vulnerable; encourage them out of their comfort zone. Natural artists, they will innovate in whatever area they work.

Intuitive strengths: Feeling/Visual

Chapter 14
Intuition & Innocence

There's a deep relationship with intuition and innocence. Intuition works more powerfully when we come to it with a sense of wonder – that's why children and intuition go so well together. When children experience their intuition they don't question it – they accept it. They don't get into a big head trip around it. There is a simplicity that is breathtakingly beautiful and that we can learn a great deal from. Keeping a sense of wonder and innocence in your child's life can support their intuition. We can also practice this openness as we encourage our kids' intuition. The truth is, the best thing we can do is not worry about our kids' intuition. Intuition knows how to grow and expand even if we are confused about how to guide our children. It's like a seedling pushing through. Intuition will always move to make itself known.

It's also important, regardless of how many super-senses our child has, not to take intuition too seriously – have fun with it – intuition is also joyful and playful. It's there to make our life easier not harder. We can make games with it. If your child is naturally very intuitive don't let them get to caught up in it. Allow your kids to be kids. Let them get silly and dirty and be carefree, let them splash in puddles and jump up and down with excitement – at least for some of the time.

If what your child is learning and developing is not making their life happier and not fitting in to their everyday 'life' then it's not valuable and a new approach needs to be considered. With intuition don't do things for results – do it because it feels good.

Nurturing intuition takes time and patience – actually it's a life's work. Intuition grows with the child and sometimes you need to take stock and see how far they have come.

We are just the care-takers while our children are small. If we do our job well they will, as they step into adulthood, take responsibility for the care of it. Looking after intuition is a form of self love. As we respect and care for it in our children we show them how to respect and care for it themselves. It's saying 'this is important'. You are important. What you dream of, and believe is possible and we support you in this. Inevitably some children will wake into this sense of themselves quicker than others but it is not a race. What matters is that we keep them open to the potential of it, that they use it consciously however often they use it. Inevitably because our children are always wiser than us, they will grow to teach us about intuition. It's the future. It's their future.

Your children are not your children.
They are the sons and daughters of life's longing for itself.
They come through you, but not from you,
And though they are with you, yet they belong not to you
You may house their bodies, but not their souls,
For their souls dwell in the house of tomorrow
Which you cannot visit,
Not even in your dreams...
You may strive to be like them,
But seek not to make them like you.

- Kahlil Gibran, 'The Prophet'

References

Barker, Robin, *Baby Love*, M. Evans and Company, Inc., 2002

Choquette, Sonia, *Vitamins for the Soul*, Hay House, 2005

Ray, Paul H. & Anderson, Sherry Ruth, *The Cultural Creatives: How 50 Million People Are Changing the World*, Three Rivers Press, 2001

Xue, Charlie C.L., Zhang, Anthony L., Lin, Vivian, Da Costa, Cliff & Story, David F., *The Journal of Alternative and Complementary Medicine*, 2007, 13(6): 643-650

About the Author

Julie Hamilton is an intuitive therapist, columnist, author and Destiny Editor for *Woman's Day* – the biggest national weekly magazine in Australia. She is also a regular guest clairvoyant on both 2DAYFM and NOVA radio.

Julie works extensively with children, teenagers and adults, one-on-one and in seminar, as an intuitive therapist, to help them uncover their personal passion, so they can live their dreams, build their self esteem, explore their creativity and achieve their highest potential. She believes that being able to access our inherent intuition is the key to personal happiness and fulfillment, and that we can teach ourselves and our kids how to do this by using simple techniques.

A motivational speaker, Julie presents regularly at conferences and on national radio covering her twin loves – mind/body/spirit and children. She also facilitates workshops for parents and carers of children on how to bring children up in touch with their intuition, so they can make great choices for themselves.

As a journalist and a health professional she has written about children, families and the issues they face for eight years in three best-selling publications including, *Australia's Parents*, *Mother & Baby* and *Practical Parenting* magazine. Julie is currently Editor of a national magazine for children aged 8-12 years. Her first audio series for children – adventure visualizations, to help kids unleash their intuition and imagination – are available on CD from New World Music.

When she's not writing, teaching or speaking, Julie looks after her greatest inspiration, her two beautiful and very noisy boys.

Also available from Blue Angel Gallery

Meditations for Kids by Kids
by Jarrah, Tahnaya, Ky & Jessica Wynne
ISBN: 978-0-9757683-6-5

In this touching collection of meditations, the Wynne children - Jessi (age 11), Ky (age 9), Tahnaya (age 7) and Jarrah (age 4) - have created a book to uplift, inspire and nurture kids of all ages! Beautifully illustrated by the Wynne children and presented in full-colour, this is a book you and your children will treasure!

"These words and pictures will take children away from the rush, bustle and harsh realities of the world, opening up a world full of imagination that is endless, safe and full of love. It will encourage them to connect with their feelings, release their fears and worries and provide them with some coping strategies in these days where beauty and innocence are so often forgotten."
- Helen Schweiger, Pre-school Teacher

Meditations for Children CD
by Elizabeth Beyer & Toni Carmine Salerno

Help your children to enter the world of their imagination through these inspiring creative visualisations. Designed for primary school aged children, these guided meditations will help kids tap into the magic world of their creativity and spirit. For use during the day or at night, this series of meditations will calm and relax as Elizabeth and Toni's gentle and reassuring voices take them into their imaginations-where all is possible! (7 tracks. Running time: 48 mins)

Books

Mercurius:The Marriage of Heaven & Earth by Patrick Harpur
ISBN: 978-0-9802865-8-8

The Secret Language Of Your Body by Inna Segal
ISBN: 978-0-9802865-5-7

Beyond The Emotional Roller Coaster by Anthony Salerno
ISBN: 978-0-9802865-1-9

Animal Dreaming by Scott Alexander King
ISBN: 978-0-9803983-0-4

Angelic Inspirations by Toni Carmine Salerno
ISBN: 978-0-9757683-5-8

Goddess by Toni Carmine Salerno
ISBN: 978-0-9757683-8-9

The Philosophers' Secret Fire by Patrick Harpur
ISBN: 978-0-9802865-2-6

Toni Carmine Salerno:Art, Life, Reflections by Toni Carmine Salerno
ISBN: 978-0-9579149-4-0

Oracle Card Sets

Ask An Angel Oracle by Toni Carmine Salerno & Carisa Mellado
ISBN: 978-0-9757683-2-7

Animal Dreaming Oracle by Scott Alexander King
ISBN: 978-0-9802865-3-3

Angels, Gods and Goddesses by Toni Carmine Salerno
ISBN: 978-0-9579149-6-4

Crystal Oracle by Toni Carmine Salerno
ISBN: 978-0-9579149-8-8

Guardian Angel Cards by Toni Carmine Salerno
ISBN: 978-0-9579149-7-1

NOTES

NOTES

NOTES

NOTES

NOTES

NOTES

For more information
on any Blue Angel Gallery release,
please visit our website at:

www.blueangelonline.com